Hope you enjoy -
Patricia Kuhn

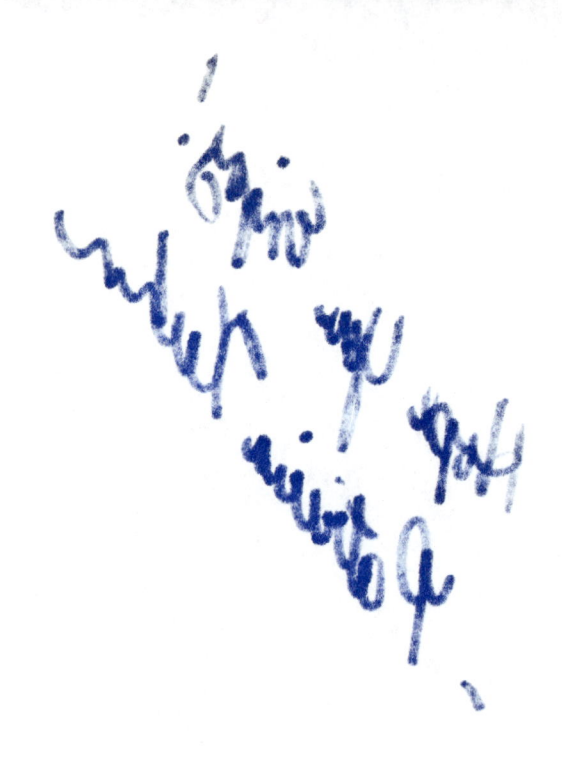

Will I Live, Will I Die?

© 2008 by Patricia Kuhn

All rights reserved

Reproduction of this book or any part thereof is prohibited, except for quotation for review purposes, without express permission of the author and publisher.

Printed in the United States of America

ISBN 978-0-9799474-7-6

SeaStory Press
305 Whitehead St. #1
Key West. Florida 33040
www.seastorypress.com

Will I Live, Will I Die?

Patricia Kuhn

SeaStory Press
Key West, Florida

This book is dedicated to my family
and friends, who supported me
through my ordeal
and continue to stand beside me
with love and courage,
and to organ donors and their
families who give unselfishly
The Gift of Life.

Patricia Kuhn

Chapter 1

I LOOKED UP AND SAW MY FATHER STANDING OVER ME WITH A gun aimed down at me. I screamed at him to not shoot me and I moved over to the center of the bed but the gun went off. I didn't know if I had been shot or not. My father ran out of the room and I heard another shot. Then I heard him running out of the house and the door slamming. I heard my mother, two younger sisters and brother all screaming or crying and I wondered if he had shot one of them. I told myself to wake up.

I thought I was dreaming because I did relive the experience of my father shooting at us from time to time in my sleep. I told myself to wake up again. But it didn't happen – I did not wake up, though I kept repeating "wake up, wake up." All my life when I had nightmares like this, I was strong-willed and could tell myself to wake up, that I was having a nightmare, and I would instantly wake up. I guess my waking life was nightmare enough, and I had decided that I would have some control over my nightmares when sleeping.

When I realized that I was not going to wake up, I kept thinking *Where am I? Why can't I just open my eyes? What's happening to me?* That was the most frightening moment of my entire life. I realized I had no control whatsoever. These were the first thoughts I had when I realized that I was absolutely not going to wake up. I understood that I must be very ill. The nightmare was happening right at my bedside and I was experiencing a grave life-threatening medical crisis. I could hear people talking, but I couldn't see them. I couldn't move. I kept screaming, "I'm right here. Can't you see me? Can't you hear me? Please help me." I kept trying to think of what must be happening to me. My thought process was slow, like pouring honey from a jar. I couldn't think a complete thought, just a few wisps here and there.

Then it seemed that I found myself lying on a beach with my youngest sister Karen. It was just like watching a movie and my sister and I were actresses in it. We were lying there sunbathing, talking and having a good time. I sat up and looked around, but there was nothing but desert behind us and ocean in front of us. It was so surreal. Then I heard a "whoosh," and I could feel intense heat sweep over and past us. I looked back and could see the mushroom-shaped cloud of a nuclear bomb. I realized that we would have a chance to live only if we could find shelter. I look all around, and to the left of us I see what looks like a cement dock in the water about twenty yards offshore. It looks as if there is a door with a handle cut into the cement, and it looks as if you could pull up the door. I am hoping that there are steps leading somewhere.

Karen runs with me to the water's edge and we start wading hand-in-hand. When the water starts getting deeper and deeper, Karen looks at me in horror and tells me what I have forgotten, that neither one of us can swim. I tell her to stay where she is, that I will get there somehow, and I will get help and come back for her. I cannot swim very well because of traumatic incidents that left me with a fear of the water. I almost drowned as a child, and later when I was in swimming class in college, I was called out of class to be told that my grandfather and eight-year-old cousin had just died – from drowning. I did not return to the class, but I had learned enough to be able to swim underwater, so I dove in.

Suddenly, I am someplace else, and Karen is not with me. I am lying on something cold and metallic. I try to move, and I realize that I must be tied down. I open my eyes but all I can see is darkness. I hear voices approaching. As they come closer all I can see are orange outlines of people's bodies. I know then that I am in danger; I am in a very evil place, where even color does not exist. I feel nauseous and very, very hot.

Then I hear my mother, Carol, talking and she sounds as if she has been crying. My fiancé, Bill, and my sister, Debbie, are talking and I hear him tell her that she must not sound upset when she talks to me, that she must sound positive. I know they are coming closer to me because their voices are getting louder. I try yelling at them to tell them to get away, to get out of this evil place, for I think that they are in danger too. I know they cannot hear me screaming, because I cannot hear myself. I realize that I must have lost the ability to speak. They come near, and they are all telling me, one by one, that they love me, and that everything is going to be all right. I did not hear Karen's voice. Where was she? *What are they talking about?* I ask myself. I want to warn them to get out of this horrible place. Then as suddenly as they were there, they were gone. I didn't even get to tell them that I loved them too. I realize that I must be dying for everyone to be so upset, and I must be in a hospital or some other type of medical facility. Even though I had these thoughts about dying, I had no idea how right I was or how close to dying I really was.

My thoughts then shifted to my son, Shawn. I wondered where he was, because I had not heard his voice at all. I could feel my thoughts drifting away, and I tried hard to reach out and embrace and keep just one of them with me, but I couldn't. Sometime later I was able to start thinking again. I must figure out where I was and find a way to get out. I kept repeating to myself the one idea that got me through the bad parts of life I had experienced since choosing to go into foster homes at the age of fourteen, and then on my own at the age of eighteen. I said to myself "You lived with your father for fourteen years and if you could do that and survive, you can get through this." This was my motto and I tried always to live by it. I decided that I would not let myself forget it now, but cling to it for strength.

I then seemed to realize I was not alone. There were other people; it seemed like we were in hospital beds. I tried talking to them, but again could not hear myself saying the words. Like me, they must not be able to talk. *Okay* I realized, they weren't going to be any help. I must determine where I was. *Okay,* I remember I was on a beach with desert behind me, and a nuclear bomb went off. Maybe these other people were on the beach too. I could hear water now. So I must be someplace under water. *Oh, yes,* I must have made it to the cement dock, and I'm in some underwater facility. But I know it is an evil place, where I cannot move or speak. So, why are they keeping me here?

And Karen, what happened to her? She must be dead on the beach, because I must have made it to the dock, but was brought down here before I could get someone to go back and help her. Maybe Karen is one of the other people around me. If she was not brought to this facility, I don't know if that is good or bad, because I feel the worst sort of agony being in this place and not being able to get out. It was like the same dreadful agony that you feel when you are told that someone that you love has died. Then every morning for a long time after that, when you wake up, it hits you in waves all over again. You can't run, you can't hide and it sweeps over you again and again.

It seemed like only a few seconds passed, then I hear Karen telling me that she loves me. Even though I can't feel it, I know she is holding my hand and she sounds like she's okay. *Good,* now I feel so much better because I don't have to worry about her. She seems safe.

I tell myself to think rationally and to figure out what exactly is happening to me. I obviously must be very sick and really close to dying because of the way my family is talking. It has to be a hospital or some type of medical facility. Before I can rationalize any further, I feel myself uncontrollably drifting away again. I force my thoughts to go back to when Karen and I were on the beach. I decide that we must have been on some military base, and a nuclear bomb went off by accident, and the government is hiding some of us who were affected by it in this underwater facility. That way no one will know the mistake that they have made. I decide I must appear to cooperate and not understand what they have done until I can find a way to escape. That should not be hard, since I cannot move or talk.

Then I find myself somehow standing outside my first grade schoolroom and I am six years old again. *What am I doing here,* I ask myself? This can't be real because I know that I am an adult. I can't remember how old I am but I know I am much older than six. I look down and see the beautiful dress and shoes that I am wearing. I remember that I had been dreading going back to school that day. I did not want to see my teacher, Mrs. Heart because I had not been in school for two weeks and she would want an explanation.

My mother had tried to take me and my sister and brother and leave my father. She had taken us to Ohio to her sister; only to find out that her sister had become a violent alcoholic in the three years since my mother had last seen her. It was just as bad living with her and her husband as it was with my father, so we had to come back and now I had to explain to my teacher where I had been. *Why am I thinking about this* I ask myself. Maybe it's because we were trying to escape my father when I was six and now I am trying to escape whatever is happening to me in this place.

Next I am transported back to my third birthday party. My father had put together a bike with training wheels for me for my birthday. I could see that bicycle so clearly. The birthday party was starting out as one of the happiest days of my life. Everyone was smiling and having a good time. We were having ice cream and cake, and I had gotten a lot of presents. After the party, my father went to the bar, got drunk and came home and threw my bike in the street, where the wheel was run over by a car. He accused me of leaving it in the street and he wouldn't fix it for me. A week later, a nice boy from across the street tried to bend it back into shape so that I could ride it. My father saw this and told him to go home and mind his own business.

That was the first time that I said to myself, "I hate him." I was reliving that experience as if it were happening all over again. It seemed so real, but I knew that I could not possibly be three again. I tried to rationalize it. *Maybe* I tell myself, *it is to remind me that even at three years old I had to be tough and I really need to be tough now because I am probably facing death.*

I know I should quit thinking about and reliving the past, and try and help myself now, to determine what I can do to survive what is actually happening to me. Maybe I can keep from dying. Even though this is the way that I want my mind to go, I uncontrollably go back to when I was five years old and our house is on fire. My father tells me to run for help and I am running through the smoke and I run to the end of the street to the house of a man who is a fireman. I figure he would be the one to help me most.

Maybe I am recalling these awful memories to get myself to come up with a strategy that will get me out of what is happening now, like the strategy I used as a child to get to the fireman because he could help me most. My mind wanders to thoughts of my grandfather who was the one person who always tried to protect me when I was a child, but he was not here to help me now – I realized I was alone wherever I was and could only rely upon myself.

I must be reliving these childhood experiences for a reason. Maybe I was thinking about giving up on trying to escape. Maybe I was comparing my mother's situation to my situation and realized that there was no one for me to turn to and it was hopeless. *No,* I told myself, *you are not going to give up!* In looking back, and as strange as it may sound, I believe that it if I had not lived through such harrowing experiences as a child, I would have died at exactly that point. I think that many people going through such a severe medical crisis would have given up then and given in to death because it would have been easier. Lucky for me that I had childhood experiences to form the foundation that made me a very strong person.

Suddenly, I can feel myself going back to the darkness and I am still telling myself to wake up when a bridge appears in front of me. I somehow know that if I can just get across the bridge, I will be okay. I see other people walking across the bridge, but they seem Like shadows. I decide I must get behind them and follow them across. It is only a few yards away from me, and then just a few feet away. I must get there. I see other people starting to cross the bridge, but I can't make it even to the edge of the bridge. Nothing is restricting me but I seem to be moving in slow motion and it seems to take such a long time to go forward even a foot. Before I can get there, the bridge vanishes right in front of my eyes.

Chapter 2

CLIP, CLIP, CLIP. I CAN HEAR THOSE SOUNDS VERY LOUDLY, AS they were being made right at my ear. I seem to be looking down from the ceiling, and I see myself lying on a bed. Everything is black and white – there is no color. The clipping sounds I hear are two people cutting my hair off. "Stop! Stop!" I scream, but they must not hear me because they don't even look up. I don't want my hair cut. It has always been very long and that it how I like it. Why are they doing that? It doesn't make sense to me. I was just at a bridge and now I am looking down at myself.

Then I hear one of the people talking, and I know that she is a nurse by what she is saying. She is telling the other nurse that she has to buy and bring in her own hair conditioner for washing and combing patient's hair that is long, like mine, because the hospital's products don't work. She is trying to show them that they need to buy products like the one she is using. But I want to tell her, "Forget about the stupid hair products, look at what you are doing. You are not just combing my hair; you are cutting it off. You are making a mistake. Please stop."

Again, I realize that they can't hear me and I think they can't see me either. Then I hear a scraping sound. Scrape, scrape. It just keeps getting louder. What does she have in her hand now? It's a razor, and she is shaving my head. I try to move closer to the table and to grab her hand and take the razor away, but I can't move. I tell myself not to worry, that my hair will grow back. But I still don't understand why they are cutting it.

What is happening to me? What is going on? I'm beginning to feel that I just can't handle this. One of the nurses turns my head to the side and I can see my head and I can see that only one half of it is shaved. I wonder why they shaved only one half. That looks worse than shaving the whole thing! I also see that my eyes are closed and I wonder if I am already dead and just looking down at myself before my spirit moves on.

Then I am in another room and I can see myself lying on a table and there are many people around the table. I realize that it is an operating room. *What are they doing with that knife? They're cutting my head open. Why would they cut my head open? Am I dead and they are doing an autopsy or if I am not dead, am I having brain surgery?*

Everything is still black and white except for the blood and it is so very red. *Are they cutting into my brain? Wait! They have stopped cutting. Look at all the blood.* It just occurs to me that I must be either dead or dying, because I cannot get back to my body. I cannot feel any pain. All I can do is look down at my body. This seems so scary, yet so fantastic. On television I had seen people who said this had happened to them, but I never believed them. I asked myself what could have caused this? Was I dying of the radiation on the beach? I told myself not to panic; it was possible I was still dreaming but somehow unable to wake up.

I don't know why I cannot feel what they are doing to me. I look down. What are they doing now? They are putting something else in my head. Now they are stitching up the cut. They are bandaging my head. What could they possibly have put in my head? It looks as if I have a miniature straw sticking up out of my head and they are leaving it there. This is definitely becoming more than I can handle. I believe that I must get away from this; I must escape this. The thought forms, but then I feel myself slowly drifting away once again. It seems that I cannot wake up, but I can go to other places. As I drift, I think I hear submarine sounds. I really must be underwater.

It seems like just a short time, and then I am lying on a cold metal shelf once again in that terrible place. I look up and see a man gazing down at me. I try to talk and am surprised to find that I can. I ask him who he is and he replies that he is an orderly who works there. Amazingly, I can see colors. First it was just black with orange outlines for people and things, then black and white and the red of my blood, and now I see colors again. I did not understand at the time that seeing colors was a positive thing.

I am trying to tell the orderly that I need to escape, and asking him to help me escape. I tell him that I will give him all of my savings. I tell him that I will give him everything that I have. He said that he would think about it, but as far as he knew, it would be impossible, because we're in the middle of nowhere in the ocean in a hidden facility. The only time someone came or left was by arrangement and scheduled transportation by boat or submarine. People who worked there were only allowed to leave every three months and then for only two weeks. He said they had signed contracts stating that they would never reveal where they had worked or what their jobs had been. I had been hearing submarine sounds and wondering if there was another way into the facility besides the door in the concrete dock. Now I knew there was another way: under water, by submarine.

The next memory that I had was the orderly coming to my bedside and whispering to me that he had figured a way out to get me out of the facility, if I felt I was strong enough to do it. I didn't feel strong enough to do anything, but I was going to try. He said the garbage and sewage from the facility were sent through an expulsion system, through a large tube, onto a particular part of the same beach where my sister and I had been. At selected times workers would come and cart the garbage and sewage away. He said that he could stretch-wrap me and put me in the sewage expulsion system, and it would shoot me up to the beach. He would put a knife in my hand so I could cut myself out of the stretch-wrap once I was on the beach. He would come and get me half an hour before the scheduled expulsion time, and I would have a total of one hour of air within the stretch-wrap, so I had one half hour to cut myself out and get away before anyone saw me.

He made me agree that if I did escape, that I would never tell anyone that he had helped me. I gave him my phone number so that he could contact me when he was on leave and I could pay him. He said that if I did not pay him he would contact the facility anonymously and tell them where I was, so I assured him that I would pay. My escape was to be the next night at about the same time. Then I started counting to 3,600 over and over again, because I figured that represented one hour. When I had counted 3,600 twenty-four times, then he would come back to get me.

I eventually fell asleep, and he never did come back. I heard the nurses talking about how he had been found dead. Word had spread around that he had been killed because he was not loyal, but was planning something that could possibly cause civilians to find out about the facility, and all the programs would have to be aborted.

They said his body had been taken up to the beach for his family to claim for burial. They would be told that he had died in the line of duty. It very painful, knowing that I had such a great part in his death - that it had been my fault. I vowed then that I would not ask or involve anyone else in trying to escape from this horrible place.

Sometime after that I heard Shirley, one of my co-workers talking. She was saying, "Can you hear me? Hang in there. You're going to be all right. Everyone at work misses you and can't wait until you come back. Even your boss misses you." I had to chuckle over that, because my boss and I never did see eye to eye about some of my duties, and now he misses me? I wanted to say, "Ha, Ha, you are really funny." But I could not talk. Then I thought, "What is she doing here?" Even though I could not feel it, I somehow knew that she was holding my hand, just like I had known that my sister Karen had held my hand.

Suddenly, I knew definitely that I was not in the same reality that I had lived in for forty-two years, but that I had moved into another reality or time, and that I had to find my way back. I kept thinking about Star Trek, and how they sometimes ended up in different realities. I tried to recall how they had gotten back to where they belonged, but I just couldn't remember.

I am so cold – so very cold. Why are they pouring and wiping cold fluid all over me? And I feel as if I am totally nude. Once again, I am looking down at myself from above. I am on an operating table again. Many, many people are around me. They all look so serious. They all appear to be saying a prayer. One of them has a scalpel. *Oh no, please don't cut me again. Please don't cut me with that.* Why are they cutting me? They are not cutting my head now. They are cutting my body. They start cutting me all the way down my chest. They keep cutting. And cutting. I think I know now; I understand. They are using my body for experiments. They are using me as a guinea pig. But when my friends and family come to see me, or should I say "my body," I am covered with a sheet and they can't see what has been done to me. I must figure out a way to tell my family so they will get my body out of this place. And then I will find somehow, some way to get back to my body. But if they keep cutting I will not have a body to go back to. Then where will I go?

What are they doing now? Oh no, they have cut me up and down my abdomen and now they are cutting me across my abdomen. This looks just like the cut they make on a cadaver when they are doing an autopsy. Now they are taking something out of the right side of my body. What is it? Is it one of my kidneys? Are they selling human organs for organ transplant? I remember that one of the ladies at work had come in and requested a family medical leave to help take care of her mother-in-law who was dying of liver failure. She said she was on a waiting list for a liver from someone who died but that organs were hard to get because not many people were organ donors and that her mother-in-law would probably die waiting. At the time I thought, "Wow, her mother-in-law must have been an alcoholic for her liver to be failing," and that's about all I thought of it. In less than a week, my co-worker had returned to work; her mother-in-law had indeed died waiting for a liver transplant. At that time I had not given it much thought at all but now I thought that maybe they were cutting out one of my kidneys because there was a shortage of parts. Maybe they were cutting it out and selling it to people who would die if they did not get one. That would mean that I was definitely dead, and just had not moved on yet. That must be why I was not feeling any pain when they were cutting me. I felt sad because I did not want to be dead. I really wanted to be alive.

My thoughts went to when I was ten years old and in church where there was a little girl who had to be on a dialysis machine every day because her kidneys were failing. I wondered how long she had lived. I don't think that transplants were being done at that time, so she probably hadn't lived long.

I was thinking, "Maybe I should be glad that I am not in my body because it would be terrible to look at myself and see all the cuts and stitches and scars." I knew then that if I was still alive and my body was not rescued they would probably cut my other kidney out and that would kill me. I knew you could not live with both of your kidneys gone. But wait, what are they doing now? They are putting something in my body where they cut me open and took something out of me. It looks bigger than a kidney. They took it out of a metal bowl before they put it in me. What are they doing to me? I have to figure it out. I just have to. First they put something in my head and left tubes sticking out, and now they're putting something in the right side of my abdomen. This reminds me of the show *The Bionic Man*. Have they put sensors in my head and replaced some of my organs with bionic ones? Is that why I can't think clearly? Is that why I'm out of my body – because something foreign is in my head affecting my brain and my thoughts. I told myself, "I need to rest for a while. I need to rest my mind for a while. I don't want to see what else they're doing to me. I've got to rest, and then maybe I'll be able to figure a way to get out of here."

Chapter 3

THANK GOD, I FEEL LIKE I AM BACK IN MY BODY AGAIN, BUT I have an intense pain in my abdomen. I don't want to feel the pain, but maybe that means that I am alive after all. Then I remember that they have cut me open and taken something out of me and then put something back in. I see a doctor standing over me and she is asking why I am in the facility. I wish I could tell her, but I cannot talk again. She takes the bandages off my head and chest and looks in shock at what has been done to me. I keep trying to get her to look into my eyes so I can somehow tell her how they are cutting me and using me as a guinea pig. She yells for the nurses to come to the bedside and she asks them what I am doing there. Not one of them has anything to say. They look alarmed that she has found me in the facility and is looking at my cuts. I am afraid to look at my chest, but I must. Before I can though, she puts the bandages back on me. She looks into my eyes and says to me, "Don't worry, I realize that you are not supposed to be here, and I will schedule a submarine to come and pick you up tonight. Don't be afraid, you won't be here very much longer."

I can feel my heart racing with the excitement that I have been found and will be rescued shortly. How beautiful this person was. This is how an angel must look. I decided to try to sleep and to get some energy in preparation for leaving that awful place. I say to myself, "Wow, I am sleeping a lot. I think I'm sleeping more than I'm awake." The submarine is getting closer. The sound of it is getting louder and louder. I must try to remember to tell the doctor that I want to go to a major hospital so they will be able to find out all that has been done to me. They will be able to see what is missing and what has been added to my body.

Okay, I think, although I am back in my body, I still can't talk. What have they done that prevents me from talking? Will the hospital be able to repair what they have done to me? Now I can see the doctor coming. She looks down at me reassuringly, as if to say, "Everything will be all right." She pushes my bed down a long hallway and into a small room. The sound of the submarine is getting louder and louder. Suddenly two men come in to the room and grab the doctor. She struggles with them and says, "What are you doing? What are you doing?" but they are bigger and stronger. They turn her around to face my bed, and one of them pulls her head back, and in front of me, cuts her throat. Blood is spurting all over me: In my face, on my body, all over the white sheet. The other man picks up the phone on a wall and says, "Please turn back, we don't have a pick-up after all." Then the sounds of the submarine became weaker and weaker until I cannot hear them anymore. One of the men picked up the doctor's body and went through a doorway. I heard a splashing sound. They must have thrown her body into the water. I felt such horror. It was beyond belief. But I was sure that it must be true, because I was not having a nightmare and I could not wake up. I was actually living in this hellish place. The other man standing there looked at me and said, "Two people have died for you. How many more before you just accept that you are here for good?" "Never!" I screamed to myself, "I will never accept that. I will get out of this dreadful place. Somehow. Some way."

They are all around the bed and I am tied down. My mother, my two sisters, my son, and my fiancé are there. I try to talk and I find that I now can. I ask them how they got there. Bill explains that they came on his boat and tied the boat up on the top of the facility that's just a little bit above water, and they came down many steps to get to where I was. I try to remain calm and not get hysterical, so they will take me seriously. I tell them, "Look, you all know me. You know when I'm serious and when I'm not. So believe me when I say that you must get me out of here immediately. Look in my eyes and see the agony, and understand that you must believe me, and only me; not what anyone else in this place says. I cannot say more, because I will endanger you all. So, please pick me and carry me up the steps, and let's all get out of here."

Bill says that he can't do that. I reply that he is 6'6" and weighs 220 pounds, and that I am 5'8" and weigh 140 pounds, so why can't he? He says that it's not because he can't do it physically, but because I need to stay there and do whatever the doctors say to do. At that point I did something that took everything that I could muster up within myself to do. I begged. They all looked at me sadly. Then they simply turned around and left. At that point, I intensely disliked my fiancé and my family, and I had never before felt that way about any of them. Even though I now know that what seemed to be happening was not real, the memory remains strong.

Then I look up and see a doctor. I suppose he's a doctor, because he has a white coat and a stethoscope around his neck. I hear a paging system say "Paging Dr. Alex Tanner to the Emergency Room" and he leaves immediately. So that must be his name, Dr. Alex Tanner. He comes back in what seems like a short time. I ask him to please let me go, to stop hurting me. He said that he was going to let me go, but first he is going to perform a procedure on me to disguise me so that no one will know who I am when they release me. To my horror, he says he is going to change my DNA from a woman to a man. I can barely breathe and I am feeling hysterical. I tell myself that I must remain calm. He must be joking, but he looks totally serious. I close my eyes and try to pretend that this is not happening to me. I try to envision being a man and being able to live with that, but I can't, because I love being a woman. I've always been glad I was not a man. A nurse put something over my nose and tells me to count backward from one hundred. I try to get up to get away, but I realize that I can't because I am tied to the bed. Darkness is rapidly closing in on me. I am screaming for help, but I know it is futile, because there is no one there who can or will help me.

I feel myself being pulled away from my body once again. I am looking down on what looks like an incubator for babies, but it is an adult size, and there is someone in it, someone totally nude. Oh no, I can't believe it, but it is me in the incubator, and I'm shocked to see that I do not have hair, any hair, anywhere on any part of my body. I ask myself if they have changed my DNA to a man already and shaved my head to make me look more like a man. But no, look; I don't have any hair anywhere on any part of my body. What have they done? Are they going to release me like that? "Do I feel like a man?" I ask myself. No! I think I still feel like a female, but nothing in this awful place is as it appears to be, so I don't know for sure. I then see my body in the incubator move into the fetal position. "How can that be?" I ask myself. My mind is up here, and I am looking down at my body, so how can my mind be telling my body what to do. I feel such terror, but I realize that I cannot give up trying to find a way to get back to my life, to get out of this terrifying dimension. For that is what I still think is happening. I have somehow gone to another dimension or reality. I feel myself drifting off into something like sleep. It is actually a relief.

It can't be! I think, and I see Princess Diana seeming to float toward me. She is dead; she died in a car accident. But here she is in front of me and she starts talking to me. She tells me that I must go back, that I must raise my son. She says that she did not get to finish raising her sons but that I can if I do not give up. I try asking her how I can get back to him. I tell her that I do not want to give up, but I do not know what to do. She slowly floats backwards away from me, and I can hear her say "You must focus and you will know what to do, you can go back; it is not too late."

Slowly the awful realization comes to me that I must be dead because she is dead. So how does she think I can go back if I am dead? *No, no* I think, *it can't be. If I am dead, am I one of the spirits that are caught between this world and the next?* No, I will not believe or accept that. What did she mean about my knowing what to do. I try to concentrate and focus on how to get back to my reality. I suddenly and instinctively know that I must die from this reality and go through some type of transference to get back to living my own reality. That is what they do in science fiction movies. The word that worries me the most in that last thought is "fiction." Then I decide that since I do not have any better ideas I must will myself to die, in order to get back to my son, family and friends. I put all my concentration to accomplishing this dreadful goal. I can feel myself floating around in darkness. I see an even darker void in front of me with a tiny speck of light in the middle of it and I know that I must get through it and to the light and come out the other side in order to live. I prepare myself mentally to go through it and I plunge into the total darkness.

Chapter 4

THE NEXT THING THAT HAPPENS IS THAT I HEAR A VOICE SAYING, "Please try to wake up. Your family is here to see you." I open my eyes and see one of the kindest faces that I have ever seen. It belongs to a nurse. I try to talk but realize that there is something in my mouth stopping me. I try to pull it out, but before I can, Bill grabs my hand and tells me to not do that. I was still angry with him for not rescuing me when I had begged him to get me out of this horrible place so I snatched my hand away. The nurse comes over and tells me that she will have to tie my hands if I do not stop reaching for my mouth. I realize that I can feel it when she touches my hand. She tells me that I have a breathing tube in my throat and that she would like to take it out to see if I could breathe on my own. *Yes, I shake my head, yes, please take it out, so that I can tell you what is being done to me.* I think that I must be in a different part of the facility. Maybe this is the legitimate or unhidden part of the facility where they are actually there to help you get better. If the nurse who is looking down at me is with the others who have done wrong things to me, then she is a good actress. The main thing that I can think about is that my DNA has been changed to a man. She can find a doctor who can change me back to a woman. All they will have to do is to test me and they will see what has been done to me. They have the ability to do sex change operations so they should be able to change my DNA back to a woman and reverse any physical changes. This is all that I can think about because I know that something very basic in me has been changed.

The nurse says that, as soon as a doctor comes, she will take the tube out. I say a prayer that it will not be Dr. Alex Tanner. If it is, then I will know that I am still in the same part of the facility. A doctor comes in and, thank God, it is not Dr. Tanner. The nurse asks me if I am ready, and I nod *yes*. She tells me to try to cough. I do, and she pulls the tube out.

At first it seems okay, but then I find that I am having difficulty breathing, and I try to tell them, not realizing that they have already left the room, so they can't see that I am struggling to stay conscious. My family, however, can tell by my eyes that something is wrong. I must find a way to tell them. My hands are free, so with my fingernails I try to carve the word "air" on my leg. They don't understand. They think I'm trying to hurt myself and try to hold my hands down. I feel myself gasping for breath. Karen finally realizes what is happening and runs out of the room to find a doctor or nurse. The same nurse comes back in and explains that she must put the tube back in. At that moment, I must have fallen asleep or passed out, because I do not remember what happened next.

I wake up again and I realize that a tube is in my throat again. A nurse comes in and asks if I want to try having the tube removed again and I nod *yes* that I do. A doctor comes in and removes it, but puts oxygen tubes into my nose. I inhale deeply. It feels so good to be back in my body. "Now" I tell myself, "I must tell my family exactly what has been done to me, so they can find a doctor to change me back to myself." I try to talk, but the sounds coming out of my throat are deep rasping sounds with no recognizable words. The nurse asked if I want pen and paper so I can write down what I want to say. I nod my head *yes*, and she brings it to me. But I can't get my hands to do what my mind is telling them, and the words look like gibberish written down.

The nurse tells me that I must try to rest and sleep, and eventually I will be able to talk and write again. For some strange reason, I somehow feel safer. I don't think that any harm will come to me, or to the nurse who is helping me – not like the orderly and doctor that they killed for helping me. Also, my family and fiancé are with me all the time now, so they can see if anything wrong is being done to me. I wake up again. A different nurse is there this time. She tells me that I need to try sipping a little water, so that it will help my throat so that maybe I can talk. I try to pick up the cup of water, but I am so exhausted that I cannot lift my hand. The nurse leaves and comes back with my mom and my sisters. She tells them that they need to feed me ice chips to soothe my throat, so that I can attempt to talk. My family keeps telling me that I have been in a coma and that God has saved me and let me live. It may be true that I was in a coma, but a whole lot more has happened to me than a coma. That is probably what this facility has told my family. A few hours later, I'm able to talk. At least I think I am talking until my family tells me that I am starting a sentence but not finishing it. For example, I think I am saying, "Get the military police to come here so I can talk to them." All that is actually coming out is "Get the military." Since I think I am still in an underwater military facility, I want them to get the military police so I can tell them what Dr. Alex Tanner and the others here are doing to me, so they can get help. I try saying the sentence in small fragments: "Get the" then "military police" then "to come to see me."

Karen rushes over to one of the nurses and tells her what I have said. I hear the nurse tell my sister to just go along with what I'm saying and pretend that she is doing what I'm asking, just to keep me calm. *Oh no, I think some of the nurses here are in on what the doctors are doing to some of us patients.* I watch Karen as she comes toward me. She pats my hand and says, "Don't worry Patty, I will go and call the military police for you right now." She pulls the drapes around my bed. I look down at her feet and she takes a few steps outside the drapes and just stands there. After a minute or so, she comes back around and through the drapes and says, "Okay, I called them. They should be here in a few minutes." I look at her and realize that she is either in the conspiracy with the doctors and nurses or has let them talk her into believing that everything is normal in this facility. Either way, I cannot control my temper, and say to her, "God will punish you (pause) for not (pause) believing (pause) me." When I finally get this out, her eyes well up with tears, and she runs down the hallway crying hysterically. Debbie says, "Don't worry Patty, I believe you, and I will call them right now." I watch her feet as she walks around the curtain and down the hallway. I then hear her tapping in a phone number and saying, "Yes, I am with my sister in ICU, and she needs you to get the military police up here to talk to her." She says, "Thank you" and then hangs up. She then comes back to me and tells me that I need to try to relax while I am waiting for them to arrive. *Thank God someone believes me.* I feel myself drifting into sleep.

When I wake up, my entire family, my mother, my two sisters, my son, and my fiancé are all around the bed. I ask where the military police are, and Karen tells me that I don't need to talk to them because I am all right. I scream at them brokenly, "If you (pause) took me (pause) away when you (pause) came to see me (pause) before by boat (pause) my DNA (pause) would be the same." They just look at me in astonishment, thinking *what is she talking about?* I ask Debbie, "Do I look (pause) like a man?" And she replies that I could never look like a man. Shawn takes my hand and tells me that I am definitely a girl. But his eyes tell me that something is just not right. Bill has an imploring look on his face, and I ask him what is wrong with him. He says that he just wants me to eat, that it has been one-and-a-half weeks since I have eaten. I tell him "Fine," just to get him to leave me alone. He tells a nurse and a while later a tray is delivered to the bed. It has bouillon, Jell-O and a Popsicle on it. Bill helps me sip a small amount of the bouillon by holding it up to my mouth. He feeds me some of the Jell-O and cuts the Popsicle into small pieces and feeds it to me with a spoon. The Popsicle is the only thing that tastes good to me. I suddenly feel extremely nauseous, but I keep trying to eat.

Everyone is thrilled that I have eaten all of the Popsicle. The nurse looks in and when she finds out that I have eaten all of the Popsicle, she tells my family that they can bring more, and I can have them whenever I want to help keep me hydrated. Suddenly none of this makes any sense to me. I feel very confused. I am feeling overwhelmed and I just want to be alone. When my family asks what kind of Popsicles I want, I tell them banana; only because I haven't seen banana Popsicles since I was a child, and I figured it would keep them busy trying to find them. I could be alone, and not expected to eat, not to try to talk, just have some solitude so I could try to think of a way to get out of this place. Obviously not even Debbie believed what I had been trying to tell her. Who had she called when she said that she had called the military police for me? She was not going to help me get out of this place. No one is going to help me. It worked about the Popsicles and everyone was talking about different places they could go to find the banana Popsicles, and all of them were soon gone.

    A nurse came in and turned on the TV in the corner. I was trying to stay awake, so I concentrated on the programs. I did not want to go back into the darkness again. *Strange* I thought, that these were the same shows I had watched as a kid: *McHale's Navy, Petticoat Junction, Gilligan's Island,* and shows like that. The television station was TV Land and I had never heard of that one. I tried concentrating on the shows, but each one seemed to be about death and dying and torture. Funny, I don't remember those shows being that way when I was younger. Then *Fantasy Island* came on, and when the host appeared, he looked right at me and said, "See the light up above you and to the right of you?" I replied "Yes," I saw it, but it was above another curtained area. He said, "That light is your lifeline, and if you don't get up there before 2 a.m. tonight, you will die." He then went back to talking to the guests who had come to his island for their fantasy. I kept yelling, "Nurse, nurse" until one came over to see what was wrong with me. I asked her to please help me get up to the light and I repeated what the host on *Fantasy Island* had said. She said that another patient was inside the drape, and the light was above her, not me, so I could not go up to the light.

    I lay there the rest of the evening and into the night trying to will myself to leave my body again and go up to the light, but it didn't work. When I wanted to get back to my body, I couldn't. And now when I wanted out, I couldn't get out. Later in the evening I thought I heard one of the nurses say that she wished she could go to the other patient's house and into her root cellar, and she would be able to find out how the patient had been poisoned. At 1:45 a.m. I saw a nurse go into the curtained area and yell for a crash cart. I could see people rushing in and trying to resuscitate the patient. At 2:05 the doctor pronounced the patient dead. I lay there anticipating that I would be dying at any moment, for I had been told that it would be me dying. Why had she died, and I hadn't? At 6:00 a.m. I was still alive.

A short while later, a group of doctors surrounded my bed and asked how I was feeling. I did not answer them. I just turned my head away and ignored them. During the day, my family came back with a cooler of Popsicles, but I did not eat any. I just felt hopeless, because no one would listen to me or believe what I was trying to tell them about what was happening to me. During the last few days I had been taken many places for what seemed to be many different kinds of tests, and no one had tried to harm me any further. *Good*, maybe the bad doctors and nurses were done experimenting on me and torturing me for a while.

A male nurse came to my bed that night and said that he needed to talk to me and asked if I would be willing to listen to what he had to say and consider that he would be telling me the truth. I nodded *yes* because I was interested in hearing what he had to say. I was having a hard time concentrating on any one thing for very long, but I was willing to try. He must have understood this because he said that he really wanted me to pay attention to what he was going to tell me. He had talked to my family, my fiancé, my co-workers, and all the doctors and nurses who had been involved in my treatment, and he wanted to explain everything about my case. He said that he knew that I did not really understand what was happening to me. He told me that he would make sure his other patients were okay and didn't need anything, and then he would spend the rest of his shift with me. I tried to get some sleep, but I was very uncomfortable. Not so much in pain, but unable to feel any peace. When he returned I was going to concentrate on trying to get the nurse to believe what was happening to me and to help me. He seemed sincere. A short while later he returned. He surprised me by asking me to explain what I thought was happening to me.

Wow, I thought, *Someone who wants to listen to what I have to say.* He told me to try to talk really slowly and I should be able to get whole sentences out. *Okay,* I thought to myself, *here goes.* I told him that my sister and I were on a beach, that there was some type of explosion, and that I woke up in an underwater facility. I told him about the orderly who was going to get me out through the sewage expulsion system and the doctor who was going to get me out on a submarine. I told him that both of them had been killed for trying to help me. I told him that I did not want him to die for trying to help me. He promised me that wouldn't happen. I explained that many times I had been out of my body and looking down at myself. I told him that I had watched nurses cut my hair off, shave my head, and doctors had cut my head open and put something in it. I told him about watching doctors cut me open and take my kidney or something out of my right side of my body and then put something back in. I tell him that even my family won't believe me about what was happening and get me out of that place. I tell him about Dr. Alex Tanner and about how my DNA is that of a man now, even though my body is still a woman, at least I think my body is still a woman unless the doctor went even further and changed my body also. I tell the nurse that I was in an incubator and did not have any hair on my body at all. I tell him what Princess Diana said to me and that she had reminded me that my son needed me and inspired me to be stronger. I can tell by the look on his face that he does not believe me. He is trying to hide that fact but I can see it in his eyes. *Great,* I thought, *another person who does not believe me.* I decide that I do not want to talk to him any longer so I tell him that I am feeling exhausted from so much talking and he believes me. He tells me to try to sleep and that we will talk later.

I try to turn over on my side, but I feel such intense pain down the center of my body that it takes my breath away. I remain on my back and drift off into sleep again. I come awake with the nurse patting my hand. He is trying to get me to wake up. He asks me to continue to tell him what has happened to me. I tell him that I know that he does not believe me but he tells me that he knows that some of what I tell him is true and he knows that I believe that the rest really happened. He says if I will explain everything to him that he might be able to help me. I tell him that I had finally decided to die from the reality that I was in and go through transference to get to the reality that I had always known and here is where I ended up. He tells me that he is going to explain what he has pieced together about me from talking to everyone and that my fiancé and family can tell me the rest. He asks if I can remember my name and I reply, "yes." He asks if I remember my birth date, who the President is or what day it is. I have no idea what the answers are except for my name. I also do not know my home address or where I work. The nurse tells me that I was not involved in a nuclear explosion, and that I am not, and never was, in an underwater facility. He said I must have been hearing the breathing machine that I had been hooked up to and thought it was the sound of water. He said I had not been used as a guinea pig for experiments or body parts, and that my DNA is still definitely a woman.

He tells me that I was in the intensive care unit of the University of Michigan hospital, and that I had been airlifted there from another hospital. He said that a few days after being admitted to the hospital, I had slipped into a coma because my liver was failing due to a medication that I had been given. A few days after that, I had a small stroke and had to have surgery on my head and tubes put in my head to release the ammonia from around my brain that had caused the stroke in the first place. He said that when the liver fails, it forms ammonia that goes to the brain and causes it to swell up. He said that if I had not had the surgery on my head that I would have probably died from another stroke before I could have a liver transplant. He said that they had to put me on life support because my liver was failing and they were looking for a donor liver for me. He told me that this had all happened to me because of the non-steroidal anti-inflammatory medication that I had taken for inflammation in my wrist and for carpal tunnel. He said that a donor liver had been found at the last minute, that I had had a liver transplant, and that now, days later, I had finally come out of the coma. He said that if I could not get my mind to encompass what had really happened then I would not get better — that if I did not truly understand what had happened that I could not get through the recovery from the transplant because it would take everything that I had in me to survive.

I could not remember any of this so I explained to him that it was really hard for me to believe. It seemed so far-fetched. I asked him again if I could please talk to the military police. He replied that this was not a military facility, so there were no military police. He offered to get the hospital Chief of Security to come and see me and I could talk to him. I replied that I wanted him to do that. I wanted to believe the nurse, but as a test, I asked to talk to the Chief of Security. The nurse told me to try and get some sleep and the Chief of Security would come and see me in the morning because he worked day shifts. I couldn't sleep. I just lay there for what seemed like hours. I tried to think about what the nurse had told me but more and more, I was having a hard time thinking. It was pretty quiet for a long time and suddenly I hear doors open with a swish. I can hear a lot of men talking. The bed I was in was directly across from a nurse's station and to the left were the two large swinging doors that the men had come through. They walked past me and started going from bed to bed, spending a little time at each one. I realized that they were all doctors. I looked at each face to see if Dr. Alex Tanner was one of them, but he was not among them. I decided that I was not going to talk to anyone until I knew for sure where I really was and what had happened to me.

When they came to my bed, they were reading my chart and called the nurse over who had been with me most of the night. One of the doctors asked me what my name was, but I did not answer him. He then asked if I knew what day it was. I just turned my head away from them because I was not going to trust anyone yet. Another of the doctors asked the nurse if I could understand what they were asking. The nurse looked at me and said, "Please talk to them and let them know you understand what has happened to you." I just ignored them and closed my eyes. I heard the nurse tell them that I had talked to him for two long periods during the night, and that maybe I wasn't responding because they had given me a large dose of the anti-rejection medication and a steroid. One of the doctors said that he had hoped that I would have made more progress. The doctors moved on to the next patient. The nurse came to the side of the bed and said that the head of security would be there soon and I would understand where I was. Not too long after that, a man in a uniform walked up to the bed and introduced himself to me as the head of security for University of Michigan hospital, Ann Arbor, Michigan. I asked him if Dr. Alex Tanner was on duty, and he replied that there was no such doctor on duty, nor was there any doctor with that name at that hospital. He said that he knew that I was confused about where I was, and he gave me his business card and told me that I could call him anytime that I felt something was not quite right, and that he, or one of his staff, would come right away to see me. Then he left.

I saw the nurse who had talked to me the previous night at the nurses' station, and I can hear him telling the others that he is going off duty, but to please let all my family members and fiancé see me, and to tell them that I was disoriented and that they needed to keep telling me what had really happened. He came over and told me that he would see me that night. I tried thinking about everything that everyone had told me. I felt so overwhelmed. I could feel tears welling up in my eyes and pouring down my face. *Quit crying* I think, *you must be calm and try to rationalize what is happening.*

"Do you believe the nurse?" I asked myself. And the security guy, he could be anyone dressed in a uniform. Maybe this is all a conspiracy to hide what they have done to me. A nurse came over to take my blood pressure and check the medicine in my IV. I ask her if she knows when my family is coming to see me. She said that they are in the hospital, that they are staying at the Med Inn, which is the hotel in the hospital. She said that she would call them to come and see me. "A hotel in a hospital?" I asked myself, "That doesn't seem right either."

Chapter 5

WHEN MY FAMILY ARRIVED, MY MOTHER WAS IN A WHEELCHAIR. I briefly thought about asking her why, but immediately decided that it must be something negative and I didn't want any more negativity. My family was happy to see that I could talk better than the day before. They told me that the nurse had told them to explain to me exactly what had happened to me. My younger sister, Karen, said that she would explain what had happened because I had confided quite a bit to her in the last six months. She said that she needed to go back to the last three years to explain what had happened. She asked if I could remember working. I told her that I could vaguely remember an office. She explained that I had been working at the same company for twenty years and for the last twelve I had been working with computers as a Computer Project Manager.

She said that about three years ago that the company had downsized and let a lot of the employees go, therefore most of us were doing two jobs. She said that my typists had been let go, and I was doing my regular job during the day and typing at night. She said that I had worked like that for at least six months, when one morning I woke up and couldn't move the upper part of my body. She said I thought that I had had a stroke. She said that I had to yell for Shawn, who called 911, and I had been taken to a local hospital. She said that they diagnosed me as having an upper extremity nerve breakdown. My shoulders, arms and hands were damaged. The hospital released me the same day, but told me that I had to see my primary care physician immediately.

When I went to see my primary care doctor, she told me that I needed to contact my employer and tell them that I could not at present work using my hands, but I could work verbally. She said I had nerve problems in my shoulders and neck and had carpal tunnel affecting my hands and tendonitis in my wrists. She told me to tell them that they should contact their worker's compensation company because I would need surgeries in both my hands and wrists and physical therapy for my neck and shoulders. Then she sent me upstairs to another doctor in the building for a second opinion. That doctor totally agreed with her.

When I contacted my employer, they said they would call me back. I had told them that I really wanted to continue to work and asked if they could get the typist back for me. When they called me back, they asked that I go to a doctor selected by the worker's compensation company. I went to that doctor and he not only agreed with the two previous doctors, but also said that if my employer wanted me to continue to work, they would have to provide transportation to and from work, since he would not allow me to drive because my hands were so bad. He would not be responsible for me having an accident and hurting myself and/or others. To my sister's surprise, my employer talked a co-worker into picking me up every day and dropping me off every evening. It was actually a good thing for both of us because I was limited to forty hours a week and therefore the arrangement was beneficial for the gentleman who picked me up. He picked me up every day for a month.

I kept asking my employer when worker's compensation was going to approve my surgeries and physical therapy because my hands were hurting worse and I wasn't even using them. My employer responded that worker's compensation wanted me to go to yet another doctor. That doctor told me that I did not have carpal tunnel, tendonitis, or nerve damage in my neck in shoulders, but that I had fibromyalgia. She then sent me back to work with no restrictions whatsoever and said that I could drive myself back and forth to work. Although I was doubtful that her diagnosis was correct, I felt that whatever fibromyalgia was might be better than the other diagnosis. Then I went to the University where I had gotten my degree and pulled up as much information as I could from their computers. I found out that in order to be diagnosed with fibromyalgia you must be experiencing some type of pain in at least eleven of twenty-one pressure points in your body. Karen said that I had called her and discussed this at great length because I only had five painful points: one in each wrist, and one in each shoulder, and one at the base of my neck. I made an appointment to go back and discuss this with the doctor. I went to my appointment and met with the physician's assistant who comes in first to find out why you're there, and I told her that I was there to discuss the doctor's diagnosis. She excused herself from the room and said that she would be right back. When she returned, she said that the doctor would not see me, that she declined discussing her diagnosis with me. I didn't know what to do at that point.

A co-worker told me that I needed to get an attorney. I called one and got an appeal started. I asked the attorney what I was going to do about working with no restrictions, because using my hands was making them worse. The attorney explained that unfortunately if I did not do the job without restrictions, my employer could let me go. Therefore, Karen told me, I went back to work and had to continue using my hands. She said my primary care doctor sent me to a hand surgeon who agreed with the three previous doctors that I needed surgery on my hands and wrists. When six months had gone by and my worker's compensation trial was to begin, I received a letter from worker's compensation telling me that they would pay for my surgery and that I would receive compensation for the time I had to spend off work.

Karen said I had been relieved to finally get something done. She said I scheduled my first two surgeries, one for carpal tunnel in my left hand and the other one for tendonitis in my left wrist. I scheduled them for the same time, since I really didn't want to take off much time from work. She said the tendonitis surgery had worked, but the carpal tunnel surgery didn't work. The surgeon had told me that the surgeries might not work because I had worked for the previous six months using my hands and causing more damage to occur. Karen said that I went back to work two weeks after my first two surgeries. She said that I scheduled the two surgeries on my right hand and wrist just as soon as the left ones healed. After my second set of surgeries, the back of my neck where I had nerve damage became extremely painful, and I started having migraine headaches, so I was off work for two to three months. The second set of surgeries was the same as the first; the wrists were better but the carpal tunnel surgery had not worked at all. Karen said that when I returned to work and started using my hands they began swelling up, and my hand surgeon referred me to a rehabilitation center for that problem.

My sister said that I had talked extensively about the doctor at the rehabilitation center who was a real caring person and sincerely wanted to help me. She said that the doctor had sent me for physical therapy two or three times a week for my neck and shoulders and occupational therapy two or three times a week for using my hands. However my wrists had continued to swell and were painful. The doctor had asked me if I wanted pain medication, but I had told her no. She wanted me to try some nonsteroidal anti-inflammatory drugs in order to get the swelling down. I agreed to take those, but I just did not want to take any pain medication.

The doctor started me out trying different medications, but nothing seemed to help. I had been off work for quite a few weeks and really wanted to return to work, but couldn't with my wrists swelling up all the time. One day the doctor had called and asked me to come to her office and to pick up some samples of a new medication that she said had helped a lot of people with my problem. I drove to her office and picked up the samples. I tried them and by the next day all the swelling was down in my wrist and the pain was gone.

The doctor had told me to please call and let her know whether the medication seemed to work. It had seemed to be working almost too well, because I overall felt better than I had in months. I had called Karen and discussed this with her. She suggested that I talk to the doctor about it. I called the doctor the next day and repeated the well-known adage: "If it seems too good to be true, then it probably is." My doctor responded that no one thought that penicillin was such a great drug when it was first discovered but look at all the new medicines that were derived from it and all the good that it had done. That seemed to make sense to me. I didn't know how wrong I was.

I asked her if I could return to work on the following Monday. She said that yes, she would give me a return-to-work slip and called the pharmacy with a prescription.

I went to my pharmacy to pick it up, but they said that it was not on the approved medication list of my worker's compensation company, and that I would have to call them to get it straightened out. I used my cell phone and called from the pharmacy. When I talked to my representative concerning it, the only question he had was, "Can you return to work now?" When I assured him that I could, he asked to speak to the pharmacist and gave the approval. I started taking the medication and returned to work.

That doctor had also referred me to another doctor who was injecting a cortisone-type shot in my head once a month as a treatment for the migraine headaches. Karen said that the rehabilitation doctor was very sick herself. She had had cancer and a mastectomy and she was going through treatments during the time that she was treating me. Karen said that I had felt very sorry for her because she seemed too weak to work and had lost her hair and seemed very uncomfortable wearing the wigs. My sister told me that the doctor had confided in me that she didn't feel like working but that she had to in order to keep her Blue Cross plan so she could have reconstructive surgery for her breasts.

The surgery had been approved for the doctor and she had turned my treatment over to the doctor whom she referred me to for the cortisone shots in my head. I could very vaguely remember having my hands in casts. I looked at my hands and wrists and could see the scars from all the surgeries, but I could hardly feel my hands at all. Karen said that I had told her that I only had about thirty percent of the feeling left in my hands. I said, "I can hardly feel them at all, Karen, like there is no feeling left." She said that she was going to leave for a while and let me get some rest and that she would be back later to talk to me some more. Suddenly rest seemed like a very good thing and I gave into it.

Chapter 6

LATER IN THE AFTERNOON MY SISTER, DEBBIE, CAME TO SEE ME. She asked if I could remember any of the events that Karen related. I said I was trying, but that I was having a hard time remembering the immediate past and that I could not remember much at all about anything earlier. I did see the scars on my hands so I supposed it must be true that I had had the surgeries. Debbie said that I had not talked to her very much about what had happened to me, but that she had talked at great length to my co-workers and especially to a lady who had worked for me at my business.

"My business?" I asked, "I have a business? I cannot remember anything about a business." Debbie excused herself at that point and went to the nurse's station, and I could hear her tell them that I could not remember a lot of really important things, like owning a business. The nurse told her that they were afraid that I had suffered some memory loss and that they would eventually be giving me some neurological tests to find out how severe it was. She told Debbie not to dwell too long on things that I couldn't remember, because it might upset me and they really wanted to keep me calm. It amazed me at how good my hearing was, yet my memory was barely there at all. When my sister came back, she did not mention the business and I immediately forgot that she had said anything about it.

About this time, my mother and Karen came to my bedside, and I could see that they had both been crying. Karen was pushing my mother in the wheelchair. I decided I needed to know why, so I asked her. She looked at me in astonishment, and then tears filled her eyes. She said "Don't you remember taking care of me?" "I don't have any idea what you are talking about," I replied. She told me that two months previously she had had a hip replacement and that I had taken two weeks vacation from work and had come to West Virginia to take care of her. I could not remember any of it. I could see Debbie shaking her head at my mother as if to say, "Don't talk about it anymore."

Debbie said that the people I worked with had told her about some pretty amazing changes that had taken place with me starting about six months ago. They said that I had started coming into work extremely tired and without make-up and sometimes looking as if I had not combed my hair. "No way," I tell them, "You know me. I won't even go out of my house unless all my make-up is on, and my hair is always fixed." I could remember that about myself. I wondered why the people at work had told my family that. Then my mom told me that when I came to take care of her that I wore no make-up and was always extremely tired. She just thought it was because I was taking care of her all the time and that I simply didn't have time to put the make-up on or do my hair. She said the only time I had for myself was when she was sleeping and then I would go to sleep also.

My co-workers told my family that they would page me for a phone call and I wouldn't respond. They would come looking for me and find me standing in a corner in the bathroom just staring. The PA system was right above my head, but I was unaware of any of it. Although I was usually so sharp and alert, I had become overwhelmed with my job and didn't seem to be able to concentrate. They said that they would find me asleep at my desk and that had never happened before in the twenty years I had worked there. I had always been easy-going but now I had become argumentative.

Karen told me that she had been taking care of my mail and I had received a letter from AAA Road Service in April of that year informing me that I could not use anymore benefits for the rest of the year, because I had exceeded my limit on services covered. Apparently I had called them many times because I had locked my keys inside the car or I had run out of gas, and a few times I called them and then couldn't remember why.

Yvonne, the woman who worked for me at my business told my sisters that usually I relieved her at 6:00 p.m., Monday through Friday, and that I worked all the hours on the weekends. *There they go about a business again,* I think, *I must try to remember it.* She said that I would get there at 6:00 p.m. and before she even got home sometimes, I would call her and ask her to come back because I was just too tired to work. She said I would take a beach towel into one of the bathrooms and lay on it on the hard dirty floor from the time that she arrived there until time to close. She said that she believed that sometimes I spent the night there when Shawn was at his father's house or with friends. She said I eventually asked her to work Saturdays for me. If she was in the area, she would stop by to check on me, and I would have my head down on my desk at the office sleeping. One time someone had stolen all the change money while I was sleeping at the desk. She told my sisters that when she asked what was happening to me, I replied that there was something seriously wrong with me but that I had gone from doctor to doctor and they could not find out what it was. When my sister said that, I had a brief memory of a doctor selling me vitamins at his office and telling me that they would make me all better, but that is all I could remember.

Karen told me that there was a lot of paperwork at my house from many doctors that I had gone to seeking help in the last six months, but no one had found anything except high enzyme levels in my blood work, indicating a problem with my liver. The doctor had made a note to monitor these to see if they were increasing.

Chapter 7

MY FAMILY SAID THAT BILL WANTED TO COME IN AND TALK TO ME and explain some more things about what had been happening to me for the last six months. Then some hospital people came in to take me somewhere for some tests. It seemed as if the technicians were constantly trying to get blood out of my veins, but many times they were unable to because my veins were so small and hard to find; when they did find one sometimes it would roll. I felt so alone. I asked my family if they could come with me for the tests, because I didn't want to go with these people I did not know. The nurses said that it wouldn't be necessary for them to go with me and I couldn't believe that they didn't argue but went along with the nurse. As they were walking out the door, I asked my family to simply let me have some time alone for a while.

When Bill came to see me he said that the nurses had told him that I did not remember anything that had happened to me and that I still thought that I was in a place where harmful things were being done to me. He repeated that I had been in a coma and that must have been when I thought all the terrible things were happening. He said that I had been sick for at least six months and that I had gone from doctor to doctor trying to find out what was wrong with me. My co-worker Beth had finally figured it out through a newspaper article. She asked to speak to me privately in the conference room. I had assumed that she was quitting because the company was having a big turnover at that time, but instead she said that she had something to tell me, and that I should sit down. She had a newspaper article for me to read and then she said that I should call my doctor. Bill said that I had read the article and immediately called him and told him that many people in other states had died of liver failure from the medication that I had been given. They had died in a shorter period of time than the time that I had been taking it. I told him that the article said that the medication was intended to only be taken for ten days, for such things as pain from a root canal. Bill had told me to call the doctor immediately.

—

When he said that, a flood of memories came back. I shook my head at him to stop talking because I did not want to be distracted and stop the memories. I was really glad to be having them. I remembered Beth telling me about the article and I also remembered calling my primary care doctor and telling her that I thought that I knew what was wrong with me. She had said to fax the newspaper article and my last blood work to her, and she would call me right back. I remember I started crying silently, sitting at my desk at work, tears streaming down my face. I went to the fax machine and faxed the information to my doctor. Just a few minutes passed and she called me back and told me to get to her office immediately. She said, "Just get your purse and your keys and get in your car and get here. I'm going to have the lab downstairs stay open to analyze your blood work." I found Beth and asked her to please tell my boss that I had to leave immediately for a medical emergency.

I called Bill on my way to the doctor and told him what was happening, but I told him that I knew then that

I was very ill and it was probably too late for me to survive. He told me to calm down and call him when I got to the doctor. When I arrived, the doctor went to the lab with me and explained the urgency of taking and analyzing my blood. She stayed with me until the results were given to her. She told me that she had been watching the enzymes in my liver since my physical a few months ago, when they showed slightly higher than normal, but that they had not been high enough to cause liver failure. I remembered when the lab delivered the results and the doctor looked at them, she then said, quite emotionally, for me to go and sit in the waiting room and she would find a specialist for me to see immediately. She found one who would stay open and wait for me. He was half an hour away. She put the newspaper article and my lab work together and told me to show him those and my actual medication. I drove to his office and showed him everything. Amazingly, he sold me vitamins from his desk for $80.00 and told me that they would decrease the enzymes in my liver, and not to worry, that I was not going to die from liver failure. I remember asking him why my primary care doctor was so concerned and he didn't seem to be. He said that he was a specialist and she wasn't; she really didn't understand all the details

    I recalled telling the doctor that Bill and I and our children had planned to go to Cedar Point, an amusement park, and then on farther to West Virginia for a week, and did he think I needed to cancel the trip, in case the vitamins didn't work and that I might need to go to the hospital? He said no, that I was perfectly fine to go on the trip. I, however, did not feel perfectly fine. I called my employer and told him that I was sick and needed to take a couple of sick days off previous to my vacation. By this time, my boss knew about the newspaper article and said,

"No problem." I called Bill and told him what the doctor had said.

I started taking the vitamins twice a day, and went to bed for the next couple of days. I called the lady who worked for me at my business and asked if she would start filling in for me a couple of days sooner than she had planned to for my vacation. I didn't tell her what was happening, just that I didn't feel well. She and I had become good friends, and I did not want her to worry. I was too tired to pack and really did not want to go on the trip, but Shawn was so excited about it that I made myself get out of bed and get our clothes. When I tried on clothing for the trip, such as shorts, tops and bathing suits, I realized that none of them fit me. I usually wore loose-fitting suits to work, but I had noticed lately that they were a little tight too. I called Bill and asked him to go with me shopping, because I had no clothes that would fit me, and I really did not feel like driving. Amazingly, for a man, he enjoyed going clothes shopping with me, but seemed quite concerned when he realized how swollen my abdomen was. After shopping, I filled a cooler with ice and snacks, and was ready for the trip.

All I remembered about the three-hour trip there was that I could not stay awake. When we arrived and checked into the hotel, all I wanted to do was stay there and sleep. Bill said that maybe it would be better for me to be out in the fresh air, and he wanted me to be somewhere in the park where he could keep coming back and checking on me. I decided to sit by the pool in a lounge chair, near the water park. He headed out with his two kids, who were eight and nine at the time, and they went to the nearest roller coaster. My son, Shawn, who was fourteen, went to the water park. They would all check in with me from time to time, and I told them that I just wanted to sleep.

After a few hours, Shawn came by and said that he thought I should get up and walk around some. He had come by many times to check on me and that I was sleeping every time. He thought I should walk around to try and wake up and that the perfect way to do that would be to come and watch him in the wave pool. When they turned on the wave action, he wanted me to see how well he did. I remember looking up at him and saying, "Well, if you want me to go with you to the wave pool, you will have to hold my hand and take me there, because I don't feel well enough to walk by myself." I will never forget his expression and I know that he was thinking, "No way that I'm going to hold my mother's hand in front of all these other kids my age around here." However, he surprised me and did not say anything except, "Okay mom, I'll hold your hand." That was when I had the most fascinating experience of my life. He took my hand and we began walking. I could not feel my feet; I could not feel my legs. I felt like I was floating. Actually, it was a wonderful sensation. I said to myself, "Wow, this is wonderful. I should ask him to run. If he runs, then I'll be flying. This is great. This feels so wonderful."

When we arrived at the wave pool I could not stand up and watch Shawn since I was exhausted from just going across the park, so he found a place for me sit down. Then he went into the wave pool, and he was having a fantastic time, and he kept saying, "Mom, look. Mom, look." I was so ill that I could hardly watch. All I could do was close my eyes, and try not to pass out. When he came out of the wave pool, he said, "How did I do, Mom?" And I lied. I had to lie. I didn't want him to know how ill I felt. I did not want him to worry. I told him how great he was, and how excited he looked, and how well he did, not falling off. Then I asked him to take me back so that I could sit and rest by the pool, because I was exhausted. On the way back, it was the same strange experience, and the same sensation of floating, of not walking, of not touching the ground.

So we arrived back at where I had been sitting by the pool, and I decided that I would take a nap. But the longer I sat there, the hungrier I became. I had an intense desire to eat. When someone would come and check on me, I remember asking them to please get me this and please get me that. Please get me anything to eat. I was having them get me things that I normally don't ever eat, such as hoagies and cotton candy. I believe I must have had every kind of food the park had to offer, and I was eating constantly. As I ate, I felt somewhat better. So I thought, *Wow, this is working because it's making me feel better. Maybe I just need to eat more.* I continued to eat on into the evening.

Then it was time for us to go back to the hotel, and to go out to dinner. At the restaurant, I did something quite abnormal for me: I ordered an appetizer; I ordered a salad; I ordered soup; I ordered the entree; I ordered dessert. Strangest of all, I ordered something that I never do eat: red meat, but I seemed to be craving it. After I'd eaten all of my food, I was also eating food from everybody else's plates, which was very rude of me, and I had taught the children not to do that. I couldn't help myself; I felt like I was starving. Back to our hotel room we had a cooler of snacks, and I continued to eat. I continued to eat throughout the night because the more I ate the better I felt, and I did not want to sleep constantly, as I had all day.

The next morning I went to where the breakfast was served at the hotel, and I got a tray and took one of everything that they had. When I arrived back at the room, everyone was pleased and happy because they thought that I had brought everyone breakfast. That was how much food I had. I had to tell them, "No, I'm still starving. You guys are going to have to go and get your own." They all kept looking at me so strangely. But they went ahead and got their own breakfast. Then it was time to start out for West Virginia.

After we were packed and ready to go and in the van, I made them stop at the vending machine, and I bought practically everything in the machine, because I wanted to be sure that I was not without food. I was so happy to discover that the more I ate, the better I felt. We left the amusement park, and we were on an expressway heading south. The night before, I prayed, "God please help me. I know there's something terribly wrong with me. I know I'm ill, and I know that I should have felt my feet when I was walking. I shouldn't have felt like I was floating. There's something very wrong with me, and the vitamins are not helping, and please Lord, please help me. Help me, because I don't know what to do."

I think that God intervened, because suddenly and without a doubt, I knew that I was dying. It was very clear to me that I did not have long to live. And I knew that I was going away soon. I knew that I couldn't control it, and that I must tell Bill, so that he could get me to a hospital. I did not want to alarm the children, so I said to him, "Please pull over." His response was, "We're on an expressway. I can't just pull over." I told him, "It's urgent, please pull over." When he pulled over, I realized I didn't have a long time to be able to talk. I had to say what I had to say, because I felt myself being pulled away. Being pulled out of my body. I said to him, "I'm very ill, and I don't care what the doctors say. I'm dying. I have to go away now. I can't stay here with you. I can feel myself drifting and unable to concentrate or talk. You need to get me to a hospital. Don't let Shawn know what's happening. Just please get me to a hospital, because I need help. Show them all the blood work. Show them the medication. Show them the newspaper article. I'm sure that's what's happening to me, my liver is failing. Please just get me there as soon as you can. Take me to Michigan. Take me to the best hospital there." I will never forget the look on Bill's face and the shock in his eyes when he realized how serious I was.

As I'm drifting away, I can hear Bill say to my son, "Shawn, could you please come up here. Your mom's just not feeling very well, and I really don't want her to go to sleep. I need to get her to the hospital so they can see what's wrong with her. Could you just make sure that she keeps talking to you. You need to keep her awake. Don't let her go to sleep." I can remember Shawn putting his hands on both sides of my face saying, "Mom, Mom, don't go to sleep. Don't go to sleep. We're getting you to the hospital." And I tried to respond, but I couldn't. I was trying to tell him I would be all right but none of the words came out. I felt as if my entire body was made of lead and I could not even move my fingers.

Next I have a vague memory of being in a hospital, in the emergency room, and handing them all the information and that was it. I didn't remember anything until I had a brief glimpse of seeing myself or feeling myself in a helicopter. Hearing the helicopter blades going around. Feeling it lift off the ground. I was thinking to myself, "What's happening? What am I doing in a helicopter?" I can remember opening my eyes and seeing a lady looking at me; she was asking questions and I tried to answer, but was unable to speak.

—

At that point, Bill looked at me and said, "You have been quiet for a long time. What's wrong? Tell me what's happening. What have you remembered?" So I explained to him that I had some memories coming back. I said the last memory that I had was of being in a helicopter.

He said that he had brought me back to Michigan and taken me to the local hospital where I had been going for treatments and therapy for the carpal tunnel and other things. Arriving at the hospital, suddenly I just sat up and said to him, "Please just let me go in here. Take my son to his dad's house. Take your children to their mother, and then come back, because I'm sure that they're going to admit me." He said that I was arguing with him; that I wouldn't agree to anything else. So, he drove me to the front of the hospital and made sure that I did get inside the door, and then he did what I asked. He took Shawn to stay with his dad, and he took his children to their mother. However, he said that when he came back to the hospital I was no longer there. They had transported me by helicopter to the University of Michigan hospital and there they did their own blood work and realized that indeed, what I thought was happening was true. My liver was failing because of the medication.

Bill said that the first hospital told him that I had walked into the emergency room, I had given them the article about the medication, I had given them the bottle of medication, and I had given them my most recent blood work, and I'd also showed them the vitamins that a doctor had given me and told me to take. And with that, they told him that I had passed out on the floor. So they were able to revive me, and they tested my blood. When they got the results, they immediately contacted the University of Michigan hospital and made arrangement to transfer me there by helicopter.

Bill said that when he arrived at the University of Michigan hospital, they told him that they were doing a number of tests on me. He said that I walked and I talked and I gave the hospital all the information. I talked to a social worker. I talked to people in the financial department. I talked to a transplant team. So for a while I was coherent and walking and talking and functioning. However, I didn't remember of that when he told me. My last memories were of being in the van on the highway on the way to see my family, and then of being in a helicopter.

On the first day and after I was admitted to the hospital and they had performed the tests and gotten the results, the doctors asked to talk to Bill and me in my hospital room. Before they could say anything, he asked "What do I tell her family? We were on the way to see them, and I need to tell them something. They are expecting us there for a week." They told him to call my family and tell them that the medication was destroying my liver. They were going to put me on a transplant list, and they would give me a beeper to wear. They were going to send me home on Monday, and when an organ became available then they would beep me and I would need to get there immediately.

They told Bill to have my family be there on Monday when I was released, and to go home with me and stay with me until my transplant could take place. He called my family and told them, "Look, you have a couple of days to get here. You need to be here by Monday. You need to stay with her until she has the transplant. She will need you there in the hospital with her when she goes in for the transplant, while she is in the hospital after the transplant and especially when she goes home after the transplant."

Bill said that they told him this on Friday evening and he had called them right away. However, he said on Saturday morning the hospital called him at home and asked him if he could come right away. He said the hospital had talked to us both together and said that things had changed dramatically and drastically and that he needed to notify my family immediately to drop everything that they were doing, and to come. The medication was destroying my liver so fast that I would be going into a coma within a twenty-four-hour period and that I would probably only live for five days if I did not get a transplant. They said to tell them to get there as quickly as possible, and that organs were hard to find, and that I might not make it. They were very clear about it. They explained to us that organs are not always available and that many people died while waiting and that they often went into a coma before dying. They wanted him to stress to my family that it was urgent for them to get there.

Bill called my family again and talked to them. He told them to drop everything and just get on the road. He said that I tried to talk to them but they were in such a state of shock that they couldn't comprehend what I was saying. He had to get back on the phone and just tell them, "Get here now. Don't question it. Don't try to figure out what's happening. Just get here now. The hospital wants you here now, because she is not going to be coherent, and you are her family, and you need to sign papers for her for anything that she hasn't decided for herself before going into the coma. They may need permission to do a number of things to her, and you need to get here now." Bill said that I was calm throughout all of this and he realized that I did not really understand what was happening.

After we talked to my family but before they arrived, he asked if there was anything that he could do for me or anything that I needed from home. He said that I made the strangest request, that I just wanted him to buy me a pair of yellow pajamas. Yellow was always my favorite color, I told him, and that I needed a pair of yellow pajamas. Suddenly I had a very brief memory of waking up in the hospital, looking down to see that I did have on a pair of yellow pajamas. I remembered looking at the hospital room, wondering why I was there. *What is happening to me?* There was a lady in the bed beside me, and she was in terrible pain, crying, and asking for help. And I remember wondering, "Where am I?" Then I remember that I had a sudden moment of understanding. In that one split second, I knew that I was dying, and I remember praying to God, "Please God, please, just let me live long enough to raise my son. He's only fourteen. His father doesn't see him a lot. I'm all he has. God please, please, just let me live long enough to raise him. That's all I ask. That's all I want. And, I promise you that I will raise him in the church and he will know all about you. Then you can take me."

Bill said that I did get to see my family; that they made it there before I went into the coma. But that all I really said to them was, "It'll be all right. It'll be all right. Don't worry about it. It'll be okay. I'm in God's hands. I tried to make a deal with him and I think he will take me up on it. He'll take care of me. Everything will be all right. I'm strong. I can pull through this." He said that I told them to quit crying, that there was no need to cry, that everything would be all right. I realize now that it must have been at that point that I slipped into the coma, because I can remember hearing my family members all crying and I remember thinking to myself, *Why are they crying? It will be all right, won't it?*

Next, I vaguely remember hearing a lady from work talking to me and I am wondering where she is. Even though I couldn't feel her touching my hand, I knew she was. I remember her saying, "Patty, it'll be okay. Hang on. We know you're strong. We know you'll get through this. You're going to be all right. You're going to get help. You're going to have what you need. Just hold on." I remember thinking, *What is she doing here? Where am I? What is she talking about? Why can't I talk to her? What's happening to me?* And then another time I recognized another friend's voice from work. I remember hearing her tell someone that she was my sister. I was thinking, "What is happening? Why would she lie and say that she's my sister? I just don't understand." Then I hear somebody say, "No, you're not her sister. Her two sisters are here. Sorry, you can't come in. Those are the rules." Then I realized that she was lying to get to see me. I remembered that she was one of my best friends. Then I heard her say, "Can somebody just tell her that I came to see her?" Then I heard someone say, "She may not be able to hear." My friend answered that she knows that I can hear because I am a fighter and if anyone could still hear, then it would be me. I said to myself, "She is absolutely right. I can hear. I can hear. Let her talk to me. I can hear her. I can't get to where she is, but I can hear her." However, they told her that they would have my family tell me that she had visited, and that maybe I would be able to hear them and know that she did stop by. Then I remember many, many people praying, and I wondered, "Where am I now? Am I in a church? What am I doing in a church?" I can't see anyone. I can just hear people praying. I can't really tell what they're saying. I seem to recognize some of the voices and in those I can hear desperation and pleading.

Bill told me that I must have been able to hear when I was in the coma, because those were things that had really happened. He said that I had slipped into a coma on a Sunday night. He had notified my employer and had also talked to my friend at work. She told him that she had tried to get into the hospital by saying that she was my sister because she wanted to see me so badly. He explained to her that he had to give the hospital the list of all my immediate family's names and they were the only people allowed to come in to see me.

    He said that the hospital had been trying to find an organ for me. He said at first they looked statewide, through the state of Michigan, searching for a liver, but could not find one. As the week progressed into Tuesday and into Wednesday, they went region-wide, which involved the states of Michigan, Indiana and Ohio. But again, there was no luck. Later in the week, they went nationwide trying to find one that could be flown in within a few hours by helicopter. He said that he had spent most of his time in the chapel praying. He said my family, my co-workers and people from the church of one of my co-workers had been at the hospital all week long, praying. That's who I'd heard praying. Their church had come to pray for me with my family and co-workers, and they were all there in the room together.

    Bill said that he had brought Shawn to the hospital, and that he wouldn't leave, wouldn't go home. He would just constantly roam the hospital, looking out windows, because he knew where the helicopter pads were. He knew that's where the organs would be coming in. Every time he'd see a helicopter land, and somebody come out with a cooler, which is what they carried the organs in, he would rush to the transplant offices or up to the counter in the ICU and ask if the organ arriving was for me.

    On Wednesday of that week, that the hospital had gone to my mother and told her they thought that I had had a mild stroke; it was due to ammonia that was being formed from my liver as it was failing and going to my brain and making my brain swell. The swelling had caused the stroke. They said that before the liver transplant, I would have to have another surgery in order to prevent another stroke that might kill me before I could have the transplant. They explained to my family that they would have to shave my head, cut my head open, drill holes in, and insert small tubes in order to get to release the ammonia. They had given me medication to dissipate it within my body, but it wasn't working.

Bill said at that time my mother was very hesitant about signing the papers, because there was always a possibility of me dying from complications from the surgery. He and my mother had gotten into a disagreement, because he thought that there was no time to lose and she was hesitating. He said that he knew she was afraid the surgery itself might kill me. Finally she did sign the papers for them to do the surgery and I came through it successfully. The hospital said that it should allow me to survive a few more days in the hope that an organ would become available for the transplant.

At that time more of my co-workers and more people from the church came and started spending time in the waiting room in the hospital. The hospital was even letting more people at one time in my room, because they didn't know if I was going to survive. He said that this also might have been the time when I was hearing them praying for me, because a lot were gathering around my bed and praying.

On Friday morning the doctors came to my family and said that they thought they had an organ, and that they would be right back to discuss the transplant and when I would be going in for surgery and what would be happening. Bill said everyone was excited and relieved, because I was only supposed to be able to live until midnight that night. Half an hour after that, the doctors came back and apologized and said they were so sorry, but the organ that was available was not the right blood type and that it would not match up with me, so it would not work. Bill asked me if I remembered everyone telling me goodbye. I told him that I was glad that I didn't because if I had heard everyone telling me goodbye, I probably would have died from a heart attack.

Bill said that a few hours before I was expected to die, he and my family were all sitting around my bed. My mother had not left my bed all day. She had been sitting there beside me, holding my hand and praying. Then he said that several nurses came rushing in and said, "We've found an organ, it's the right blood type, we need everybody out of the room. We don't have any time to lose. We don't know how much longer she has to live, and the surgery takes a minimum of five hours; we must get her in the operating room now."

Chapter 8

IT WAS ALL MAKING SENSE TO ME NOW, AND I REALIZED THAT indeed I was not in some military place where people were doing harmful things to me. In fact, a transplant had saved my life. This should have made me calmer, but instead it had an altogether different effect on me, because I started crying and could not stop. Bill tried to calm me down, but I was pretty upset at that time just realizing exactly what had happened to me, that I actually had another person's organ in my body, another person who had died. I asked him to please let me have some time alone to think about everything. He didn't want to leave me alone when I was so upset but he finally agreed because he knew that I preferred to be alone when dealing with something difficult.

The same male nurse who had been attending to me the previous day was back that night; he said that he was going to take care of his other patients and come back and sit with me and explain what I had to do in order to get better. He understood that I was beginning to remember some things that had happened. By the time he came back to me that night, I was feeling much more ill. Now I realize that I was affected by the medication and unable to think clearly for many hours after it was administered. I was somewhat normal only during the last few hours before they were supposed to give it to me again.

When he came back that evening I had been given medication an hour before and I could hardly talk. I couldn't sit up, I couldn't feed myself, and it seemed to me that I was getting worse. He said that I had to somehow find the strength to try to concentrate on what was happening, because they needed to get me out of intensive care and moved to the transplant floor so that I could continue to improve and eventually go home.

I felt queasy to know that they actually had a transplant floor and I wondered how many patients were there and if they were having as much trouble as I was recovering. I felt very sorry for them if they were. The nurse said that most patients did better at home with family taking care of them. He said that if I didn't show some improvement, I was not going to be able to go down to the regular transplant floor and then go on home; I probably would have to go to a nursing home. That certainly scared me; I did not want that. I asked him, "What is it exactly that I need to do. Tell me exactly what I need to do, and I will try hard to do it." I felt like a small child asking my mother for instructions on how to do something she wanted me to do and trying to please her. I think I felt that way because the nurse was so kind and really wanted me to get better. He said, "Look, you have to be able to sit up. Let me try to sit you up in your chair in the morning, and we'll see how you do." He told me to try to talk to the transplant doctors when they came to the room in the morning, and try to answer their questions and let them see that I was working to get better. I should let them know that I wanted something to eat or drink and show that I was trying to do my part in the recovery process. He was trying to inspire me to get better, and letting me know that I had to have the will to improve and stay out of the nursing home. I thought that if I did not begin to improve soon I would not go to a nursing home, but would probably die before getting there. A thought was lurking somewhere in my mind, almost surfacing now and then, that maybe it would be better for me to die than to feel such helplessness. I did not want to go to a nursing home. I had visited relatives in places like that and it seemed to me that people there did not get better. No matter how hard I tried to sleep, it was impossible and I kept asking the nurse to help me turn this way and that to try to get comfortable, but nothing worked.

The following morning, the nurse picked me up out of the hospital bed and put me in a chair with all the equipment around me. I tried to tell him, "I can't hold my head up, I have no energy, I hurt all over and I feel completely exhausted." He got a pillow and he propped it up beside me to keep my head from falling over and he said, "Just try. Just try to sit here. If I can just tell them that you're sitting up for fifteen minutes, they'll know that you're making progress. Try to say something to them when they come in, because they're really going to be surprised to see you sitting there and they will want to see if you understand what is happening."

When the doctors came in that morning, they were indeed surprised to see me sitting up. I will never forget the look on their faces. As I saw them coming toward me, I kept telling myself, "Say something; say something. Let them know that you can talk. Let them know that you understand what's happening." All I could manage to get out of my mouth was the word "water," but that was enough to let the doctor see that I was trying. One of them rushed off and brought me back ice chips. I could not hold the cup, and I could not feed myself the ice chips, but they knew that I was coherent enough to want them, so a nurse came and helped me.

I was in intensive care for a couple more days, and I still could not feed myself and could not sleep. Either I did not have the strength to lift my hands to feed myself or I just couldn't get my brain to tell my hands how to do it. My family would come in and feed me whenever I wanted to try to eat. I was comforted by the fact that they really knew me and they knew that if I could possibly feed myself that I would. Still, because I was always so independent, it was hard to accept. I think it was a matter of pride, but I convinced myself that I had to put my pride aside or I would never recover. The medications added to the problem because when they were strongest, I could hardly think at all. On the third day, they told me that they were going to transfer me to the transplant floor. I wanted to go but I was very afraid because I did not feel like I was well enough yet. I knew I had to go to the transplant floor as a step on the way to go home, and I really wanted to go home and be with my family and have them take care of me, as hard as that was for me to accept.

Chapter 9

WHEN THEY TOOK ME TO THE TRANSPLANT FLOOR THEY PUT ME in a room with another transplant patient. The patient had not had a liver transplant, but a kidney transplant and seemed to sleep most of the time. I really wished that I could sleep too. I started having some complications at that point. I was seeing people and talking to people who weren't there and I believed some things were happening that really were not happening. A nurse asked who I was talking to, and when I told her I was talking to the lady sitting on the edge of my bed, she told me that there was no one there. She said that I was probably having hallucinations from some of my medications, or perhaps I just hadn't had enough sleep since my transplant. The nurse gave me a sleeping medication, and I lay there for many hours with the same word running through my mind over and over and over again. Then suddenly I would stop hearing that word and another word would start running through my mind hundreds and hundreds of times and I was unable to stop it. This was how I spent the first day in my room.

As evening approached I started feeling pain in my abdomen, as if someone were taking a knife and cutting my abdomen all the way across. The pain just kept intensifying. I was in so much pain, I couldn't figure out where the buzzer was to buzz the nurses, and as embarrassing as it was, I started yelling and screaming. By the time that the nurse arrived in the room, I was thrashing around on the bed, unable to lie still. It was such intense pain, I could barely breathe. The nurse immediately called for the doctors. Two or three doctors came, but they weren't really sure what to do.

They decided to send me down for tests. Being in such pain, all I could think was, *Oh no, oh no, my liver is failing. They're going to cut it out, and they're going to give it to somebody else, and I'm going to die.* The more I thought about it, the more hysterical I became. Normally I'm a really, really calm person, but just the thought that I might be dying soon was so overwhelming that I couldn't calm down. The doctors tried very hard to explain to me that would not cut the organ out of me and give it to someone else. I had learned from talking to the nurses and reading some material that they had given to me that it's very, very hard to find organs and that organs are transplanted according to blood type, so I thought the liver they had transplanted in me could work in thousands of other people, even though it wouldn't work in me, and I didn't believe what they were telling me.

They sent me to various places in the hospital for many tests, but they never could find out exactly what was happening, *at least that is what they are telling me* I thought. After about forty-five minutes, the pain started to subside and after about two hours it went away completely. When it started to subside, I told the people attending to me that it had stopped because I did not want them to take the organ away from me. I started wondering what exactly had caused it and worrying about when it would start hurting again. I decided then that I had to find a way to get out of the hospital before they could take my new liver away from me.

Later on that night, they moved me into a room all by myself across from the nurse's station. *Oh no I thought, they know I am going to try to get out of here and so they have put me where they can watch me all the time.* I did feel much better being alone; I know the patient beside me had become terribly agitated when I was screaming in pain. *This is a good thing* I thought — *there won't be another patient in the room who can tell on me when I find a way out of here.* I tried to concentrate as hard as I could on how to get out and where to go. I did not trust my family because I knew they would believe anything the doctors or nurses told them. I tried to think of which one of my friends would hide me if I could get to them. From time to time, the thought went through my mind that I was having paranoid feelings but that thought passed and I was consumed by my fears.

Chapter 10

THE NEXT DAY WAS SHAWN'S BIRTHDAY, AND ONE OF MY FRIENDS with whom he had been living brought him to the hospital with a birthday cake and presents, and we had a small party there. The only thing that I could focus on during the birthday party was a pair of scissors. My friend brought scissors to the hospital to help me wrap my son's present. I could not concentrate long enough to wrap the present so she wrapped it for me and I kept watching what she did with the scissors, until eventually I was able to get them in my hand and hide them in the tray at my bed. I wasn't sure what I would need them for but I felt safer having them.

That night they gave me sleeping medication again, but still I could not sleep. Once more I kept having the same word go through my mind over and over again, and this time it seemed to go faster and faster. Sometime during the night, I started feeling intense fear, as if someone was watching me, as if someone was just waiting to come and harm me. I decided then I should try to escape, because I believed that if I didn't, someone was going to kill me. Before I could attempt to escape, however, the sleeping pills started to work and I could feel myself drifting off to sleep. I said to myself, "This is good, this is good. The sleeping pills are working. I need to rest as much as I can so I will have the energy to escape."

A short while later, I seemed to feel extreme heat. Heat so strong that I could barely breathe. I opened my eyes and I looked around, and all I could see was jungle. I could feel the moisture of the leaves and the trees and all the jungle foliage surrounding me. I felt as if my body was suspended in some type of a hammock, as if I were suspended in the air, way up in the middle of this jungle. Then, I see four men walking on the ground, coming toward the place where I'm hanging. They are wearing fatigues and they blend into the jungle. They seem to just seep into it and to become part of it. As they approach me, it does not appear they are there to harm me. One of them says, "Please be calm, be calm. You're tangled up, and you're tied up. We're going to untie you. We can't help you get out of this place, but we can untie you, then you need to try to get out on your own. Get away as fast as you can. Get as far away from this place as you can get. Keep moving and don't look back." They then took large knives and cut me out of whatever it was I was tangled in and lowered me down to the ground.

The next thought I have is that I'm back in the hospital room and I'm standing beside my bed, but I'm hooked up to complicated equipment. I decided that I needed to get out of there, to get completely away from the hospital. I knew that I was too weak to move fast so I needed to get started as soon as possible. I needed to do exactly what those men had told me to do. I attempted to walk across the room and then remembered that I could not walk. I also realized that I had a lot of equipment hooked up to me and if I were going to walk, I would have to either get rid of it or take it with me. Then I could feel myself slipping away, and that's the last thing I remembered. The next thing that happened was that I was in a bathroom, and there was somebody pounding on the door, and I was lying on the bathroom floor. Surrounding me were get-well cards. I was just lying there as people were pounding and pounding on the door for me to open the door and to let them in. They were calling out my name, asking me if I'm okay, and asking me if I can hear them, and asking me to please unlock the door. I crawled over to the door and unlocked it, and an orderly came into the room and saw me lying on the floor. He told the other nurses he was going to have to pick me up, and for them to get all the equipment. He carried me out of the bathroom, and across the room to my bed as the nurses trailed behind with all the equipment that was attached to me. At this time, I was very clear-minded and clearheaded and asked the orderly what was happening to me and why was he carrying me to my bed, and what was I doing in the bathroom? He said he didn't know, that he would have the nurses talk to me.

After they had me all arranged and back in bed again, I asked the nurses, "What happened?" And they said that they were really not sure. All they knew was that I was in bed the last time they checked on me and then they couldn't find me. They said they were relatively new to the floor, so they weren't aware that I couldn't walk. When they inquired of one of the other nurses where I could be, they learned that I hadn't been able to walk yet. Then they checked the bathroom and discovered it was locked and realized that must be where I was. They told me to try to get some rest, that they were going to send someone to talk to me, as they felt that I really needed to try to get a better understanding of what was happening to me.

The next day when my family was in the room with me, a gentleman came in and said that he was from "A Gift Of Life" organization and asked if I would like to know the information that he could give me about the donor of the liver. He said that they were very limited in what they could tell me but that the donor was a seventeen-year-old male from Indiana. I know that I should have felt so grateful at that point and I was but mostly all I could think about was that a seventeen-year-old boy had died and I had lived because of his death. My own son was only fourteen and I could not imagine the agony that my donor's parents must be feeling. I somehow felt responsible for his death. It was a crazy way of thinking but I guess I was not thinking very clearly at all. I felt a wave of intense sadness sweep over me and I could not stop crying. My family tried to comfort me to no avail.

Chapter 11

A LITTLE WHILE LATER, A REALLY NICE LADY CAME TO THE bedside and sat down and said that she was there just to talk to me. She wanted me to try to stop crying and try to give her my attention. I asked her who she was. She told me she was a therapist and had come to talk to me because I seemed to be having a hard time understanding what was reality and what wasn't. She wanted to make sure that I understood where I was and what was happening. At that time I seemed very clear minded and explained to her that I understood that I'd had a transplant, and that I was on the transplant floor in the University of Michigan hospital, that I knew I'd had a liver transplant.

Then she asked me did I understand what had happened to me early that morning or during the nighttime? I told her that I felt myself going to sleep and then found myself in a jungle, feeling very intense heat, and men trying to help me escape. I told her that I was then back in my hospital room, and that the only thing I could concentrate on was escaping, but the next thing that I remembered was waking up on the bathroom floor with someone pounding on the door asking me unlock it. She asked me if I could explain to her what part of that was real and what part of it wasn't, and if I understood the difference. I thought about what she was saying, and I realized that there was no way that I had left the hospital room and gone to a jungle, and that there probably were no men there to save me, and that I was probably hallucinating. I explained that to her. I thought it must be caused by the medication that they were giving me, because it all happened after they gave me the sleeping medication.

I told her that at that moment, I did understand where I was and who I was and what had happened to me. She asked me if I knew my name, the date, my birth date and the president's name. The only thing that I knew was my name. I was upset that I did not know the rest of the answers, but she seemed happy simply that I knew my name and told me that she would probably be back the next day to talk to me and gave me a card and said if I needed to talk to her any time, around the clock, to give her a call. A couple of hours later, a couple of students came to my bed and told me that they were from India, and that they were here studying to be psychiatrists. They said that they would be coming around a couple of times a day to talk to me to see how I was doing and to discuss anything with me that I wished to discuss. I told them that I appreciated that, but I felt like I understood everything that was happening to me, and I really didn't need to talk to anyone. They also left me cards, just in case I needed to call them.

That night the transplant team of doctors came around; they stood outside the door and were going over my file before they came in. I guess that they did not realize that patients could hear what they were saying. I never understood that. I could always hear everything that they were saying. But this time I was really concerned, because I could hear them say, "We think she's becoming psychotic. We don't know if it's because of medication, and we are trying different medications. It could be the steroids making her hallucinate. We're not sure if she is psychotic or if it's been medication induced."

I could hear one of them say, "We need to have her watched." Another doctor said that maybe I should be put on a suicide watch. I am thinking to myself, "Suicide watch? I'm trying to survive here. I'm not trying to kill myself. I'm trying to get better, so that I can go home. Why in the world would they think that I'm trying to commit suicide?" Then I hear one of the doctors say, "Okay, starting tomorrow, let's put her on a suicide watch. Let's get the students to sit with her when her family can't, and let's not let her be alone at all. Let's not take a chance."

Chapter 12

THAT NIGHT, AS USUAL, THE NURSES CAME IN AND SAID, "We need to give you some medication to make you sleep, because you haven't been sleeping." Because they had different nurses rotating on the floor at all times, I said, "Please don't give me anything to make me sleep because I think it is making me think things that are not really happening." I refused to take it and I said, "Look, it's doing something to me. It's making me see people that aren't here. It's making me think I'm in a jungle. It's making me think people are trying to help me escape. You know, I ended up in the bathroom last night, with get-well cards lying around me, with the door locked, and I don't want to do anything like that tonight. Please do not give me any sleeping medication." However, I think now they must have put it into my IV because I could feel myself drifting off into sleep again. It was the same type of feeling that I'd had the previous night. I woke up with a start, and I thought I could see people standing there in the corners of my room, dark, ghost-like figures. They were just standing there watching me, and again, I had such intense fear that I felt I had to escape. I pushed my buzzer to summon the nurses, and after a short time, one arrived. I asked her if she could tell me who the people were who were in the room with me. She told me there was no one there. I told her they were in the corners in the shadows and I could see them and they were just standing there and watching me. The nurse assured me no one was there, that

I was safe and not to worry about it. She said no one was going to harm me. She reminded me that I was in the hospital and I was getting better. She then said to buzz again if I had any other problems.

It did not matter what she said to me because the dark figures kept staring at me, and I was panicking trying to figure out what to do. I could not figure out how to get away from them. I knew if I got out of bed, that I could not walk. I kept trying to figure out what to do. I was hooked up to all kinds of equipment on both sides of the bed and I knew I wouldn't be able to walk with all that. Then I knew what I must do. I got the scissors out of the drawer, where I had hidden them. And one by one, I started cutting away all the things that they had hooked up to me. There was an IV hooked up to one of my arms, and I cut it loose. There was a tube going directly into my liver and it was attached to a bag that was hanging down to the floor, and I cut that tube. Then I realized there was catheter inside of me, because I could not go to the bathroom on my own; I tried to pull it out, but it wouldn't pull out, so I cut it out too. I looked around me at the dark figures and they had not moved. They had not come closer to me. They were just standing there. I realized then, I've cut myself loose from everything; I don't have to pull any equipment behind me. I need to stand up, and I need to hold onto things, and I need to escape from this room to get away from these dark figures. I managed to stand up and stay standing up by leaning against the bed and holding onto it. Then I tried to decide, "What should I hold onto next, in order to get out of the room." Then I saw a chair to my right and I reached for it, and I finally made it.

I said to myself "Okay, okay, I'm making progress," but I was so tired. I had to sit down on the chair for a while. I looked around me as I was sitting there trying to decide what my next move would be and realized that I was very hot. It felt like I was lying in a tanning bed or on the beach and the temperature must be at least a hundred degrees. I couldn't stand the heat anymore and thought about removing my gown. I realized that the door leading out of the room was not that far away. If I could just get a hold of it and get a hold of the door handle, I could open up the door and escape. So I decided to stand up and try it. I made a couple of steps toward the door. That's when I felt myself falling, and I felt myself hitting the floor. Then I felt my bladder release onto the floor, and I could feel and smell warm urine all around me. I looked up, and I can see the dark figures and I realize that they are getting closer. They're coming for me. They're coming toward me. I started screaming and that is when I passed out.

I came to when people were picking me up from the floor and carrying me somewhere. I realized that I was totally nude — that I must have removed my hospital gown. They were carrying me into the bathroom, and they were putting me on a chair in the shower. They were running warm water over me, and they were telling me that they were bathing me in order to get the urine off me. They then carried me out of the bathroom and put me back in my bed.

During the next hour or so many people were coming back in again to hook up the IVs, to hook up the tube back into the liver, and to put the catheter back into me. I kept apologizing and telling them that I was so sorry, that I didn't know what had happened, that these awful dark figures were in the room with me the night before, that they were trying to kill me, and all I was doing was trying to get away, and I was trying to get out of the room, and that I understood that I had fallen down and I understood that they were re-attaching the medical equipment.

I finally comprehended that I would not be able to escape from the hospital because I was not physically or mentally well enough.

I realized then that they were tying my hands to the bed so that I couldn't possibly get up. I heard one of the nurses say to the other nurse, "You know they have on her orders for us to put her on suicide watch in the morning, but I think we need to do it tonight and get someone in here with her now. We'll keep her tied up until we can get somebody in here. We're going to have to have somebody with her around the clock from now on. We can't wait until morning." Again I'm saying to myself, and I said to them, "I heard what you just said. I'm not trying to commit suicide. Believe me, I'm not trying to commit suicide. I'm just trying to get away from the horrible people that are trying to kill me. Don't you understand that I'm not trying to commit suicide? I don't want to die. I'm trying to live." I didn't understand that my actions were endangering my own life. They told me not to be upset then, that they were just going to get people to come and sit with me. That way if I wanted to talk to someone, they would be there, and I could tell them how I felt and tell them all my fears. If somebody should come into the room that I felt was going to harm me, or if the dark figures came back, I could talk to the people sitting there me, and that they would explain to me what was happening, that they really weren't there, that I was hallucinating, that it wasn't really real. They said it would help me get through it, to please go along and not give them a problem about it. So I agreed, because it appeared they were all trying to help me. Maybe no one was trying to hurt me in the hospital. They just were trying to get me better. I tried to keep this in my mind; however, I did keep seeing these dark figures standing around in my room. I just kept telling myself that they were not real and not going to harm me. I tried to ignore them and eventually I fell asleep. I woke up at one time during the night and someone was sitting in a chair by my bed.

The next morning when I woke up, there was no one sitting by my bed. The transplant team were coming around and I could hear them talking out in the hallway, as usual. I could hear the surprise in their voices when they realized that the doctor on call the night before had put me on the suicide watch, and they were sounding quite shocked at what had happened the night before, that I was found in the floor all cut loose from all the equipment around me. When they came in the room, they asked me, "Did I understand what had happened the night before?" And I told them I wasn't sure what had happened, but there were dark figures in my room, that I had to escape from them. They all glanced at one another and one said that the dark figures weren't real. I told them that as strange and as crazy as it sounded, it was real to me. I had seen these forms, and they were trying to harm me, and that when I was on the floor, when I had fallen down, they were surrounding me. I tried to explain to the doctors that I did not need to be on suicide watch, that I was not trying to kill myself. But they told me that because of what had happened, I was going to have to have someone with me there at all times, and that they would let the nurses untie my hands, but there would have to be someone there with me at all the time, because they couldn't risk me cutting myself loose again.

That day the psychiatrist came by again and talked to me, as well as the two Indian students. They spent at least an hour each with me, so for three hours I was trying to explain to that I was not trying to kill myself. They seemed to understand, but all three kept reiterating that these things that I was seeing did not exist, they really weren't happening, that it was caused by medication, by trauma or stress, or by a mental or emotional imbalance, and that I could not give into these fears. If I felt fear, I needed to call one of them or a nurse. I had to find some way to control the fear, because I was not going to recover if I could not get this clear in my mind. The hospital was trying to save my life and prevent the liver from failing. They told me that many things could cause it to fail and stress was one of them, so I needed to calm down and concentrate on what they were telling me.

When the transplant team came around that night, I told them that I really needed to talk to them seriously, and I really needed them to listen to me. I said, "Look, I understand that I'm seeing strange things, and I'm thinking strange things, and I feel terrible fear, and I'm trying to escape from this hospital; however, you have to understand that these things are very real to me, and I think they're induced by the sleeping medication. So please do not give me sleeping medication tonight. I've asked the nurses not to, but I understand that it's probably on the orders that they do. But could you please let me have a night without sleeping medication, and I'm sure that things will be improved. These things only happen to me after I begin to feel myself falling asleep, and it does feel like the sleep is induced by medication." They agreed to try it that night, with the understanding that I had to have rest. I was going to really have to try very, very hard to sleep on my own. Otherwise they would have to give me something to sleep, because if I did not get enough rest, my body was not going to heal, and I was not going to survive this.

For the rest of that day, my mother or sisters or Bill or Shawn was there with me all the time. They took turns sitting with me so I did not need a student to sit with me until late at night. Since my family was living in a hotel within the hospital, they could each take turns. They were trying to do it all night long, but it got to a point in the middle of the night where I guess they were all so tired that a student was sent in. That night I did not sleep, but I also did not have any hallucinations, I did not see people that weren't there, I did not try to escape, and I did understand everything that was happening around me.

The next morning when the transplant team came by, they told me that they were going to send a physical therapist, and they were going to try to start exercising me and helping me learn how to walk again. They told me I would probably be really, really tired, but I needed to try to walk because that was one more step toward getting out of the hospital. They also told me that they were going to try to take the catheter out. They said if I felt like I could not control my body, then I needed to tell the nurses and ask them to put it back in again. They would really like me to have more control over my body and to try very hard to at least stand up in an attempt to begin walking again.

The physical therapists came to my room, and they managed to get me out of bed, and help me stand up, but all my limbs felt like they were made of lead. I couldn't lift my arm or my leg. They wanted me to try leaning on a walker and walking. I tried, but I couldn't take more than two steps without being exhausted and feeling like I had to lie down. They said it was a good start: that I had gotten out of bed, that I was able to lean on the walker, and that I was able to take a couple of steps. They told me if I felt able during the day, I could try starting to walk again with my family's help, holding on to the walker. That was really exciting to me, because I really wanted to get out of the hospital, and I understood that it was one of my first steps. When my family came in that afternoon, I asked them to help me. They stood on both sides of me and although I couldn't even walk from the bed to the door, I did make it half way across, and that seemed like a big accomplishment to me. I felt like I was really moving ahead; because I was not seeing people that weren't there, I was not trying to escape, I was not cutting myself loose from anything, and I was actually taking a few steps on my own with a walker.

I kept telling myself, "You can do this. You can do this. You're going to get better. You need to get stronger, but you can do this. You can survive this." That afternoon, the nurse came in, and they took the catheter out. They told me to just buzz them if I needed to use the bathroom, and they would come and help me. They said that at first we would try using a bedpan and then after that, when I felt like I could walk to the bathroom, I could go on my own. I thought, "Well this is good. In one day, we're making such progress. I'm so excited. Things are looking positive now."

However, less than a half an hour after the catheter was taken out, I could feel that I had to use the bathroom, and I could feel that I couldn't control it, so I pushed the buzzer. Before they could respond, the entire bed was soaked. And the nurses had to come in, lift me out of my bed, and replace all the sheets. They had to bathe me and put a new gown on me. I told them then, "I don't feel like I can control myself. I guess I need you to put the catheter back in." I'll never forget the male nurse looking at me and saying, "You just don't want to. We know you can do it, but you just don't want to." And I kept telling him, "Why do you think I would not want to? Why would I want to mess all over myself? Why would anyone want to do that? I just don't feel that I can go on my own yet. You need to put a catheter back in." However, he said, "No, we're going to try it without. You need to try really, really hard. Try harder than you ever have."

Within an hour, the same thing had happened again. By the time I rang the buzzer and they got there, it was too late. I tried to explain to them, "Just leave a bedpan at the bed, and let me try to use it myself, and that way the bed wouldn't have to be redone again." They lifted me out of bed again and changed the linen, and the nurse didn't seem too happy about it. It was the same nurse who had argued with me before, that I could do it. I was trying to explain, "Believe me, if I could do it, I would. If I could hold it and wait until you got here, I would." A few hours later, a nurse came back, and they put a catheter back in. I tried to explain to them that I was trying hard, and they seemed to understand. They said that we would wait a day or so and try again to take the catheter out. They said to just let them know if I felt better, then I could try sooner than that.

Chapter 13

OVER THE NEXT FEW DAYS, I STARTED FEELING MUCH BETTER. I asked the nurses, "Why do you think I'm suddenly feeling so much better?" And they said, "Well, when the transplant team comes around, talk to them and see if they can figure out what has been changed." When the transplant team came by, I told them that I was feeling better, particularly for a few hours in the afternoon. They told me that that they had decreased some of my medication, and that was giving me more clarity of mind. I was taking the anti-rejection medication every twelve hours, and the time when I was feeling so much better was the three to four hour period before it was time to take the next dose.

Then they started allowing friends and co-workers to come and see me, and that really did help me get better. My family was there all the time, but it was so nice to see other people besides my family, people that I had worked with every day. Although I couldn't quite remember what it was I had done at my job, I vaguely did remember what the office looked like. When some of the people came to see me, I had to pretend I knew them, although I didn't know them at all. Others, I did know. It seemed to be a pretty strange thing that two people could walk into my room and both of them so glad to see me, telling me that they had been working with me for twenty years; I didn't know one, but I did know the other. I tried really hard not to let anybody know that I didn't recognize him or her, because I did not want to hurt anyone's feelings.

That afternoon a couple of ladies came from where I worked, and they said they worked in the shop. They brought a collection of money for me, which really surprised me because I worked in the office and the shop did not normally take up a collection for someone who worked in the office. My family and I were sincerely appreciative of the money to help me until I could get back to work. I was amazed. It was so touching, and I did know the two people who came to give me the money. They had also brought bags of clothes for my mother, because they explained that when she was called to come, Bill had told her to simply get into her car and to not do anything but grab her purse and her keys and to get there immediately if she wanted to see me before I died. They said she had no clothes with her, and they had gone and bought her clothes. That was just so loving, that these people cared enough about me and my family to do that. I started crying again. I realized that I had cried more in the last few days than I had in the last few years. That really bothered me because I wanted to get back to being the strong, self-confident, can-handle-anything person that I remembered being. It was strange that I could remember that about myself but I could not remember my birthday or the current president's name.

After a few days, I started feeling very much better. I was able to walk around on a walker. I was still talking to the psychiatrist and the Indian students who came by to see me every day. They still had me on what they considered a suicide watch with people watching me, but I did seem to be getting better and better. One day they said to me, "You know, we think it might be better if you were home with your family taking care of you. Maybe you could make more headway that way." So, we started to work towards that.

One day they brought my medications to me in bottles, and they brought me a chart that told me what medication to take at what time. They started trying to train me to take my medication but I was unable to comprehend it. There was no way that I could figure out how to take the medication. I would look at the list and read the name of the medication; I would actually be able to pick up the bottle of medication, and then that was it. That was all I could do. I would forget what I was doing. I would start all over again. I would look at the medication list, pick up the bottle, and forget what to do. It just amazed me that I could not comprehend the simple act of taking medication. It was as if I couldn't think long enough to go through the whole process. When I asked the doctors what they thought was happening, they told me my attention span was really short, but that my family had agreed to take care of me twenty-four hours a day. They were going to let me go home, with them to take care of me, next day or the day after. Later, a nurse came along with a huge book. She asked me to arrange a time that my family would all be there with me, so we could go over all the things that had to be done when I arrived home.

I asked them that day if I could try to take a shower on my own, because I felt so dirty from not being able to have had a shower for weeks. So they had orderlies come in, and they helped me get into the shower, help me sit in a chair in the shower, and they turned the water on. I cannot express how good that shower felt. I have never before, never since, felt such a wonderful feeling as that water and soap flowing over me. And I've never felt so clean before as I did on that day. All I can remember is oohing and aaahing. They told me later that they could hear me all the way down the hallway.

I really wanted to go home, but I couldn't imagine how I would ever be able to go back to a normal life. How would I ever take care of myself; especially cooking, cleaning, figuring out how to take my medication, taking a shower without help? How would I ever go back to work, when I couldn't think clearly? What was I going to do to support Shawn and myself? The reason I was so upset about this was because of not being able to figure out what medication I was to take and when I was supposed to take it. At that time, I thought, "I must have brain damage. Possibly from the coma or the stroke. And maybe I am exhausted because there is physical damage also done by the stroke." When I asked my family if they thought I had brain damage or physical damage, they said they didn't think so, but they all averted their eyes when answering me, and I could see tears forming in my mother's eyes. I thought, "She believes I do have brain damage. I can see it in her face." I broke down. I found myself hysterically crying, because everything seemed so hard and so futile. I was happy to be alive, but was dreading what the rest of my life was going to be like with all of these impediments.

When the nurse gathered my family together to go over a number of rules concerning things that I must avoid, it added to my misery. She had brought a big manual with her for us to take home, and she was going through it. Among the many conditions, she told us: I could never be in the sunshine too long, because one of my medications could give me skin cancer; I couldn't be around children who had immunizations, because I might contract whatever disease the immunization shot contained; I couldn't go out where there was a large group of people or especially children, because I would have no resistance to any cold, virus or germ. She said I'd have to have medications throughout the day. I had to be very careful and not miss any, because it might cause my liver to start failing. She said I had to stay away from bees and avoid stings; and I had to stay away from mosquitoes, especially mosquitoes, because they carry diseases.

She told me something else at that point that I didn't know. I should have known it; I don't know why I hadn't picked up on it. She said that I would have to take medications forever or the organ would fail. She said there was never anyone who had had an organ transplant who was ever able to get off the medication. She said identical twins had actually had transplants. They thought that maybe the one who had the transplant wouldn't have to take medications for life, because it was such a good match, but she said that wasn't even true in that case. I realized then that my life, as I had known it, was over and it was gone and I was going to have to start a brand new one. The nurse said that it was not as bad as it sounded, and that I had to and would adapt.

I remember looking at her and thinking, *Easy for you to say.* I almost asked her what kind of transplant she had, to be such an authority on it, and to tell me that it was not going to be that bad. I refrained from saying it, because I knew she was just doing her job, and that she meant well. I kept feeling the enormity of how much my life had so suddenly changed. It was as if I'd gone to sleep and woken up to a totally new life. That was what the psychiatrist and the Indian students had been telling me. The transplant team had been telling me that I would be able to go back to a normal life. The part of that statement that was missing was the word "my;" they did not say that I would go back to my normal life, rather they said that I would go back to a normal life. I had gone from never, ever being sick to this new kind of existence. I reminded myself of the motto that I live by and have repeated to myself many times, beginning when I was in the coma, "You lived with your father for fourteen years, and you made it through that alive; you can make it through this." I kept telling myself that over and over again.

After the nurse left, my family and I just looked at each other in shock. I asked them if they knew before the transplant that it would so drastically change my life. They recovered from the initial shock, and explained to me that all they had been concerned about was that I live, and that they knew that I could handle anything I had to afterwards. They reminded that they all considered me to be the strongest member of the family.

After my family went home for the day, my favorite nurse came in and said that she understood that I was going to be released the next day and that I needed to remember one most important thing. She said, "Do not let them put you in a nursing home, because you will probably die there." She said to let my family, friends, fiancé, or whoever help me stay out of a nursing home. I had told her that I did not want to disrupt the lives of anyone that I knew; that I would prefer to go to a facility where people that I did not know would be taking care of me, people that were getting paid to do so. This changed my thinking, and I believed her because she seemed like such a good nurse, good hearted, and really concerned about me. I knew that she was probably right: I had to let the people closest to me help me, and avoid a nursing home.

I was determined to try to figure out ways to be able to take care of myself. I thought about it, and became obsessed with the problem of being so weak. I started trying to think of ways I could alter my home to make it easier for me. I was afraid that I would never be able to walk by myself again, or even have the energy to stand up long enough to take a shower. I paged the nurse and asked her for paper and pencil, because I wanted to do some drawings showing how I wanted to adapt some rooms in my home. She gave me a confused look, but brought me a tablet of paper anyway. I decided that I would never have the energy to go up my stairs again, so I would have to turn my TV room into the bedroom. I realized that I would have to somehow put a shower in the half bath downstairs. I proceeded to draw a picture showing a showerhead hooked to a horizontal bar installed in to the ceiling of my bathroom. It made sense to me at the time, but I now realize how absurd the drawing must have been to the nurse when I showed it to her. But she was very professional and told me that it was good to see that I was trying. She asked me if she could keep my drawing to show to my family. I later on saw her in the hallway, showing the picture to my family and telling my family that my mind was still not functioning rationally, but that it was a good sign that I was attempting to help myself get better.

Chapter 14

THE NEXT DAY MY FAMILY AND FIANCÉ TOOK ME HOME. IT WAS quite an ordeal for them because I was petrified of the sunlight. The crazy thought was going through my head about what the nurse had said about not being in the sunlight. I had no rational idea of time. I thought if they let me be exposed to sunlight at all, that I would automatically get skin cancer. No doubt about it. Therefore I would not let them put me in the car until I was fully clothed, including gloves on my hands and a hat pulled over my face. I was so panicked over this that they had to leave the hospital, go to my house, and find these things that I needed to cover myself, and then come back to the hospital to get me. I now have to give my family a lot of credit for tolerating the psychotic behavior that I was exhibiting. It must have been an amusing sight to see someone in a car, on an expressway, fully clothed that way in the middle of July.

When we arrived at my house, Bill picked me up and carried me into the house. I hated being such an invalid that I had to be carried. I can remember uttering the words, "Hurry, hurry, please hurry," because I was afraid the sunlight would touch my face below my hat. My family had my TV room set up with a bed in it for me. I realized as I watched them and listened to them that they had a plan in mind to take care of me around the clock, without me ever being alone. Karen assigned tasks and times for each person.

My mother's role was to wake me up in the morning, give me a washcloth to wash my face, take my temperature, check my blood sugar and give me a shot if necessary. Then she and one of my sisters helped me up onto the scale to check my weight. She would help me walk the few steps to the kitchen table. Karen, in the meantime, was cooking breakfast. I had to eat at least six times per day to keep my blood sugar at a somewhat normal level. My family explained to me that one of my anti-rejection medications had caused me to be diabetic. The hospital dietician had shown my sister how to chart out daily menus for me according to a special diet. She had tried to explain it to me, but she realized after a few minutes of trying to show me the booklet from the American Diabetic Association and discussing all the different food groups, that I absolutely did not have any clue what she was talking about. With the dietician's help, Karen made up a few days of menus for breakfast, lunch, dinner, and small meals in between, but she was struggling to make up new ones. At the time I don't think that she understood it entirely herself.

As I watched her sitting there and concentrating, I thought to myself, "I know something. I know something that can help her. What is it? I know someone. I can't remember who they are, but I know someone who could help my sister. There's someone who does food. The person does food in a nursing home. Who is it?" I asked Karen if she knew where my planner was and after she found it, she started reading the names out to me and then when she came to one of the names, I knew it was the person I remembered. She was the mother of one of Shawn's friends that he had known since kindergarten. I asked Karen to call her and ask if she could help plan other meals. She was kind enough to come to the house and see me and try to explain again about a diabetic diet. She was shocked when she realized that I could not comprehend what she was saying. She tried to hide her dismay, but I saw it before she could turn away from me and start explaining to my sister. She had brought with her another parent of one of Shawn's friends, who worked at an insurance company. After they helped Karen figure out at least a week's worth of menus, they got information from her concerning my insurance. My family only knew which insurance company I had, and luckily it was the same company where she worked. She said she would check the next day to be sure my policy was okay for any future home care that I might need. I was so touched by their kindness and that they took this time away from their families to help me.

While they were there, although they did look at me and talk to me, I could tell that they were pretty distressed at what they were seeing. I looked so totally different. I had caught one glimpse of myself in a mirror, and that's all I ever wanted to see at that point. Because my head had been shaved from having the first surgery, and I was so swollen up from taking the steroid, I probably looked as if I weighed fifty pounds more. I had no make-up on, and wore nothing but loose baggy pajamas because the incision site was very painful. They had never seen me like this. They had mostly seen me in work clothes either going to work or coming home from work.

After they left, my sister came and sat with me, and she tried to explain to me how she had made up the menus, so that I could understand a little bit about how I was supposed to be eating. I couldn't comprehend anything. Even though I had heard what they said to her, and I was hearing what she said to me, it didn't make sense. Now it seems so very simple, but I think I was on so many medications that I could not process any information.

Another thing my mother did was to give me various medications throughout the day. At the beginning of my recuperation at home, I had to take thirty-two pills per day. Some of the anti-rejection medications were so large that they would get stuck in my throat, and my mother would try to massage my throat from the outside to help me swallow. Many times my mother and I were afraid that I was going to choke to death. Karen later went to the pharmacist and was able to get four smaller pills, which were equivalent to one of the large pills. It increased the total number of pills that I had to take each day, but at least I didn't have to worry about choking.

For some reason, all of my senses were heightened. In particular, my sense of hearing was very acute, as if I had a loudspeaker inside my head. My bed in the TV room was near the wall behind the kitchen counter and when my sister would run the dishwasher all the clicking and clanging and water running would make me want to scream out in pain. I couldn't hear anything else. It was as if it was echoing in my mind. I hated asking her not to run the dishwasher, but I couldn't take it anymore. I asked her to please wait and run it whenever they took me to the doctor. I have to give her credit for her patience, because she didn't question me about it. Another problem was the telephone. I asked her to remove it from my room because no matter how low they put the ringer, it would just echo loudly in my brain. People would call and want to talk to me, and I told my sister, "I don't feel like talking. I don't want to talk. I can't really talk a lot, and it just so totally drains me." It wasn't that I didn't want to talk to them; it's just that I did not feel well enough. I really would have loved to talk to my friends, but what could I say to them? I did not want them to feel sorry for me, and I did not want to have to try to answer their questions.

Karen carried the bulk of responsibility of trying to help me get better. My mother and Debbie and Shawn assisted her. She made sure that I had the correct medication at the correct time, and if there were drastic side effects from any medication, then she would call the transplant team at the hospital and ask them what to do. She was truly upset when my feet and ankles were so swollen that you could not even tell where my ankles were supposed to be. The hospital instructed her to put my feet higher than my head, but she started to worry about the water going to my heart. So she was back on the phone insisting that something else be done, and the hospital called in a prescription for fluid release pills. She was out the door going to get the new medication.

She was also in charge of making me eat and drink the foods and liquids that the dietician had said that I must have. Some of the things I was supposed to eat and drink, I hated but if they were on my diet, and she couldn't find a substitute she would stand by my chair until I did consume it. Karen and my mother were normally very passive people, but they had somehow transformed themselves into active, stubborn, determined women who were going to get me better. I was amazed as I watched them go about their plan for my recuperation. They kept reminding me that I always was the strongest person they had ever known. It sounded good, but I thought I was facing an insurmountable obstacle to my recovery. I thought how unhappy they were going to be if I didn't survive. I had started to believe that I would never recover the ability to think clearly and couldn't see how I could get better.

Debbie was given the job of trying to help me walk again. She took on the role of physical therapist, and made me exercise my arms and legs many times during the day and always got me up and tried to help me walk. Another thing that the hospital had asked her to do was to have me look at a calendar each day, get me to tell her what day it was, and to get me to mark each day off. Since I did not believe that I would survive much longer, it was painful to look at the calendar and see what I believed was a future that I would never know. One time, when she became very persistent that I mark a day off the calendar, I became enraged and threw the calendar at her, and told her what she could do with it. I was so sorry just a second after I said it, because Debbie started crying and ran through my house and out the front door. I was as shocked as everyone else at my behavior, because I did not normally act like that. I was angry and frustrated because I couldn't talk very well, couldn't walk, couldn't think clearly, and, most of all, I was truly starting to believe that I would not get any better than what I was. I was actually starting to want to die. I did not want to be an invalid and depend forever upon others to take care of me.

Chapter 15

SHORTLY AFTER THIS, MY MEDICATION WAS INCREASED TO THE point that at times I did not know who I was or where I was, and it greatly affected Shawn. He would sleep on the sofa in the same room as my bed to be sure that I was okay all night. Many times I could not sleep, day or night, and I would ask my family during the day, and my son at night, "What am I supposed to be doing?" At first they did not know what I meant, but they soon adapted and would say, "You are supposed to be sleeping", or "you are supposed to be eating", or even "you are supposed to be thinking about getting better." The medication adjustment also caused a series of other problems. My doctors later told me that it probably made me more psychotic than I was when I had left the hospital.

One of the reasons that I couldn't sleep was that I started regressing back in my mind to when I was a child. In one instance I remembered that I had gone every morning before school to a friend's house that my mother had forbidden me to see or play with. I went to her door, and she and I would walk to the elementary school together. My mother said that my friend's mother had a bad reputation. I did not know what that meant and besides, I played with her, not her mother. I really liked my friend. What kept her in my mind must have been her unusual name. It was Lauralei, and her name kept running over and over through my mind and getting louder and louder. It was exactly like it was when I was in the hospital and couldn't sleep. I would try so hard to make it stop, but it just wouldn't. I would put a pillow over my head to try to make it less loud, but it didn't work. I had to wait it out, and eventually it would slow down, decrease in sound, and stop entirely. I would then try to not think at all, and that way words would not get stuck in my mind. But that didn't work. I would spend days at a time with one word going through my mind over and over again, and then another word going through my mind over and over again. It was still happening when I was eating, taking medication, trying to talk or do anything. I had absolutely no control over it.

One night when everyone had gone to bed and Shawn was asleep on the sofa across the room, a nurse suddenly appeared at my bedside. She said that she had come to give me good news. She said that the records at the hospital had gotten mixed up, and I had not had a liver transplant but a kidney transplant. She said that that was good because I now had two good kidneys — the new transplanted one and the other one that had been fine all along. She said that I was going to be perfectly healthy because even if one of my kidneys went bad, I would still have the other one, and I could live with just one kidney. I was elated at this news and couldn't wait until morning to tell my family. The nurse wished me luck and left. I was so relieved that I was finally able to get some sleep.

The next morning when my mother woke me up, I asked her to get my sisters downstairs and ask Shawn to come in from outside, because I had great news to tell them. When they were all there, I happily told them what the nurse had said the previous night. Shawn immediately said, "Mom, there was not a nurse here last night." I argued with him and told him that he had been asleep, and that he hadn't seen her. Then my sister said, "But Patti, the door was locked, so no one could have come in." I then argued with my sister by telling her that Bill might have left the door open. He would come to my house after he got off work, and he would kneel down by my bed and pray. And then he would just leave. I would lie very still and pretend that I was asleep, because I didn't want him to worry. I didn't want to disrupt his life any more than I already had.

My family explained that maybe the most recent medication change had caused me to hallucinate again, as I had while in the hospital, or that maybe I had dreamed it. I believed them, because I realized they all could not be wrong. I knew then that I was having serious mental problems, because it had seemed so real to me. I was devastated and all I could do was cry. One of my sisters must have called the hospital then, because a social worker showed up at my house later that day. She said that she could send a therapist to my house to see me, but I refused. The fewer people who saw me in this condition, the better. She was also trying to determine if I qualified for any medical or financial assistance, but I couldn't remember if I had any checking or savings accounts or any investments. I couldn't even remember who my employer was or what my job was.

Even my birthday I was unable to pull from my memory. All I kept saying was, "I don't know, I don't know. I just don't know." When the social worker was ready to leave, she told my family that they needed to go through all my records to see if they could find any information about my financial situation and she got my social security number from my mother. She said that she would be back to see me in a couple of days. I remember telling her, "No you won't, because I will not be here in a couple of days. I will not survive another couple of days.

I will be dead." Everyone just looked at me in stunned silence. Then my family walked her to the door, and I heard her tell them that they had better watch me because I might be suicidal. *That again,* I thought. I am not going to try to kill myself, I simply can feel myself being pulled away, and I just don't think that I can survive like this much longer. That night, Debbie slept in the same room with me, instead of Shawn. My hearing was still so sensitive that I could hear my mother and sister, Karen, crying upstairs and saying that it seemed like I was getting worse instead of better. "Now they understand," I told myself, "they can see what's actually happening."

Later that night I heard a helicopter and it kept getting louder and louder and it sounded as if it was directly over my house. "Hide" I told myself. "They are coming here for you. Hide. Get under the bed." I slipped out of bed onto my knees and was trying to crawl under the bed when Debbie grabbed my arm and asked me what I was trying to do and what was the matter. I said to her, "Don't you hear the helicopter? It has come here to get me and take me back to the hospital. They are definitely going to cut my liver out of me this time because I am mentally ill and therefore won't be able to survive and they will give it to someone else who will be able to survive." My sister tried to calm me down, but I didn't calm down until I heard the helicopter go away. My sister explained to me that my house was near an airport and that sometimes helicopters would fly low over my house. She tried to tell me that they would not take the liver away from me once it was transplanted in me, that it was mine always. But that didn't make sense to me because if I wasn't going to survive, why wouldn't they put it into someone else who would survive and who would be able to live because of it?

My sister helped me back into bed and she placed a stand with a TV on it beside my bed, gave me the remote, and she told me to tune to the TV Land channel to get my mind off of everything. *I will try that* I thought. I found the channel, but all I saw on the screen was dark, evil, shadowy characters killing innocent people. I tried to rationalize this by telling myself that it wasn't possible, what I was seeing, because I was watching such shows such as *Petticoat Junction, The Brady Bunch* and *The Partridge Family*. I could remember these shows vaguely, and I knew that no one was ever murdering anyone on them, that they were mostly comedies. Then I remembered in the hospital the person on *Fantasy Island* had told me that I had to get to the light in the ceiling or I would die. Then I looked at the TV again and saw one person drowning another person in a water tower on Petticoat Junction. I started screaming for someone to turn the TV off. *I am losing my mind* I thought in panic, *I am going crazy.*

My family called Bill, and asked him to please come over and talk to me, that maybe he could explain to me that it was probably the medication that was making me behave that way because it had that effect when I was in the hospital. He came over and sat down and talked to me and tried to explain that it was the medication. I was so tired of being told that. It sounded like an excuse for not telling me that I had something permanently wrong with my mind. That was what I was starting to believe and I told him so. He told me they were not sure yet if I might have some permanent brain damage from the drug that destroyed my liver, from the stroke or the coma, but that they really believed the medication was causing the current problems.

He had brought some books with him that looked like ledger books, and he said he needed to talk to me about the business. With that, Karen, grabbed him by the arm and says, "Can I talk to you in the living room?" She took him to the living room and she must have thought I couldn't hear her say to him, "Don't talk to her about the business." He asked, "Why not?" and my sister said, "Because she doesn't remember anything about the fact that she owns a business, and the hospital doesn't want her to be any more stressed out than she already is." He said, "Well what am I supposed to do, because I'm trying to keep the business open, but I don't understand how to do the books?" My sister said, "Well, you might have to close the business down, because we can't tell her that she owns it. We can't let her know anything about it at this point." I said to myself, "I wonder what kind of business I own. I think I can handle knowing. That would be a good thing. Maybe I could go back to work at my business if I can't go back to where it was I was employed before, because I don't think I'll ever be able to think very clearly. Maybe somehow I can take a part in the business that I own, or find someone else to actually manage it."

I asked Bill to explain to me what kind of a business that I had. When he explained to me that I had a family fun center, and I had birthday parties for children and had all kinds of pool tables and arcade games and pinball games, I vaguely, vaguely remembered it, but not very clearly. I definitely did not know how to do the bookwork that he had with him. So he told me that he was going to try to keep it open as long as he could, and that, eventually, if I wasn't able to go back to it, that he would have to close it up, because between himself and the lady who worked for me, they had managed to keep it going. He told me that he would try really hard to keep it open, in case I could come back. He told me her name was Yvonne, but I really couldn't remember her.

Chapter 16

WHEN I WOKE UP THE NEXT DAY, IT WAS AS IF I HAD BEEN transported back in time at least four years. Karen was saying that she needed bread. I asked her why she didn't call my boyfriend and ask him to pick some up on his way over. She looked at me strangely but did not say anything. I wondered why my boyfriend had not been over. I could not remember the last time that I had seen him. I asked my sister where he had been since he was my boyfriend and we had been together for 9 years and I usually saw him every day. I asked her to call him so that I could talk to him. My sister started to say something, but she just shook her head at me and said, "I need to call the transplant nurses and ask them something first."

She went into the living room but I could still hear her when she called and asked them what she should do if I was somehow going back in time in my mind. I asked myself what she was talking about now. I knew where I was and my name and what was happening to me. I am not sure what they told her, but she got off the phone and called my boyfriend and talked to him for a while in a whispering voice and then she gave the phone to me. I got on the phone, and I said to him, "When you come over, can you please pick up a loaf of bread? He hesitated for a couple of moments and asked if I needed him to pick up anything else. I told him that I would let him talk to my sister again about that. So he and Karen started whispering again and I heard her tell him to come over. I heard her tell him to be prepared because I was not the same person. I asked myself what she must mean by that. I knew I was ill, but a different person?

When he came over with the bread, he had brought me a basket of soaps, bath beads, bath salts, shampoos, perfumes and different things like that. He said that he had stopped by a business that a friend of his owned and that he had her make the basket up especially for me. I looked at everything and all that I could think about was that I still couldn't even walk, let alone go upstairs to take a bath. So far, all I had was a sponge bath every day that my mother gave me.

I asked him why I had not seen him for a long time and he responded that he had been very busy. He seemed very evasive and that confused me. All I could think of was why he hadn't been there to see me since I had been home from the hospital. I thought maybe he had and I had forgotten about it. I seemed to be forgetting a lot of things. Sometimes I couldn't remember what I had just said. He said that he had called various times to check on me, but that Karen told him that I was not well enough to see him. I said to him, "But you're my boyfriend. You should have come anyway. He seemed puzzled by what I was saying, but he didn't reply. I asked him if he had been at the hospital with me when I was sick. He said that he had come to the hospital to see me when he found out I was sick but he had not been able to talk to me because I was already in a coma. He said the hospital had let him in the room to sit with me for a while. I told him how good it was to see him.

He looked at Karen at that point and told her that he thought he should explain everything to me. *Great*, I thought, *what is this all about?* He explained to me that we had not been together for at least four years. I couldn't believe what he said. I felt like I was in the twilight zone because I was sure that he was still my boyfriend and couldn't understand why he was denying it. He told me that I was engaged to Bill. At that moment in time, I could only vaguely remember who my fiancé was, but I could very clearly remember a lot about my boyfriend. I knew how much he loved my son and had been a father figure to him since he was three years old. It was shocking to me that in my mind I thought it was four years ago. I felt so stupid and embarrassed. I think he could feel my embarrassment because he told me that it was no big deal because we were still good friends.

I asked my mother and sister if I could talk to him alone. I then told him that I was worried that I was not going to survive the transplant and I was worried about what would happen to my son. He said that he knew that I would survive, but not to worry because if something happened to me, he would be sure that Shawn would be taken care of. He said that between Shawn's dad and him they would work it out about raising Shawn. He offered to keep my son while I was recuperating because he said that he still saw him at least once a week. I told him that I would think about it and let him know. He said that he knew how strong-willed I was and that I needed to hang in there.

He then took my hand and he said, "Look, as you get better, you'll remember the last four years. You are having problems with your memory. As you get better, and as you progress, you will remember." I stayed confused about him for a long time. Even though my fiancé would come over, and I knew who he was, it still was very confusing in my mind. I did see my ex-boyfriend a few times after that because my sisters and my mom didn't want to leave me alone because I was having more episodes that were somewhat psychotic. When they needed something picked up, like prescriptions or groceries or whatever, he lived nearby so he would pick up things and bring them over to the house.

Chapter 17

It was about this time that Debbie decided that she was going to help me up the stairs so that I could take a shower. She tried to entice me by telling me that I could use some of the products that my ex-boyfriend had brought me. I started to tell her that I did not have the energy to take a shower, but I could see that she was determined. They had gotten a shower chair for me. It took two of them to get me up the stairs, undressed and into the shower. It was so humiliating having them undress me. It didn't seem as humiliating when my mother undressed me as it did with my sisters. I realized that my arms felt like lead and I was not going to be able to bathe myself, but I was absolutely not going to let one of them bathe me. I asked them to let me take the shower by myself and I would yell for them when I was done so they could help me out of the shower. It was all I could do to stay on the chair and not fall off into the bathtub. I was very dizzy and had to keep my hands flat against the shower door to balance myself. I knew that Debbie would not be happy until I took the shower, so I opened up the shampoo and poured some in the bottom of the bathtub so that it would smell as if I had actually taken a shower. I was so weak that all I could do was hold myself up on the chair and let the water pour over me until they came in to get me out. They were so happy because they really felt that I had progressed by being able to take a shower by myself. If they only knew the truth!

The one thing that I dreaded most during this time was that twice a week my family had to get me ready and take me to a hospital to have my blood tested to see how my transplant was doing. They would have to get me up, they would have to dress me, help me into the car, and when we arrived at the hospital, they would have to put me in a wheelchair. I was still so petrified that the sun was going to cause skin cancer automatically, that I was, wearing long gloves and long dresses. It was still in the month of July, and I always had a hat over my head.

One particular day when they wheeled me into the hospital, I saw two of the therapists who had performed occupational therapy for my hands. I did not want them to know it was me. I was so embarrassed; I was so humiliated to be going from such an active person to being an invalid in a wheelchair. So, I kept putting my head farther and farther down, so that they wouldn't see who I was. Somehow they knew who I was, and they came over to me, and it was so awful for them and me when they saw what I looked like. I tried to tell them what happened but I couldn't stop the tears that were pouring down my face. I told myself to quit feeling sorry for myself and to quit making scenes in public. My family explained to them what had happened. They said they knew something must have happened to me because I had not shown up for therapy for several weeks. They told my sister and mother that they knew the doctor who had referred me to them had given me medication that took the swelling down in my wrists, but they did not realize that it was the one that had killed so many people. They had heard about that particular drug being pulled off the market. They asked me how my hands were doing and I had to tell them that I could barely feel my hands. They had been that way since I had come out of the coma. They then told me that if the reason I could not feel my hands was because of the stroke that they also did therapy for stroke patients and for me not to worry that they could help me learn to use my hands just like I did before the stroke. I felt sad as my family was pushing me away from them and to the lab because here were two more people that I would miss should I not survive.

The people at the lab were very, very nice and they told me that they handled a lot of transplant patients, drawing and testing their blood. Each time that they took me there, I would see someone else that I did not want to recognize me or try to talk to me. I did not want to discuss what had happened and I was so ashamed of how I looked. After about my third time there and my family telling the lab people how hard it was for me coming through the lobby and seeing people that I knew, they told my family to park in the employee parking lot and bring me into the hospital from a side door. It was close to the lab where my blood was drawn. I did not dread going there nearly as much after that.

It had been a month since I had come home from the hospital, and I did not feel like I was getting any better. I still felt like I was an invalid, and I could not see where I was going to recover. I couldn't think clearly. Sometimes I still couldn't say a whole sentence. I would think the whole sentence, but when I would say it, my family would tell me that I was only saying part of it. So if I was saying, "Could you take me to the bathroom?" all that I was actually saying was, "Could you take me?" And I did not realize that I was not saying the whole sentence. I was getting so frustrated because I did not want to be an invalid, and I'd always believed that a person has a right to do what they want to with their own life.

At that time, a Dr. Kervorkian had been in the news. He had helped all these people who did not want to live.

He had helped them die. I did not want Dr. Kervorkian to help me or assist me to die, but I did not believe that I was going to survive much longer. I kept hearing my sister and my mom and my other sister talking at different, various times. Debbie had actually lost her job in Virginia because she had been taking care of me for this month and hadn't gone back to her job. Karen had left her two children with her ex-husband for the summer, and he couldn't keep them any longer, so she had to get back to West Virginia to get her kids back. My mother needed to have another surgery done, so she needed to get back to West Virginia. Therefore, I knew that in a very short time, within a couple of weeks, they would not be available to help me at all. I couldn't imagine being able to take care of myself by then.

    I came up with a plan at this point. I decided that I would somehow pretend to get better. I had to figure out how to take my medication. I still could not look at the list and read it and figure out which medication to take at what time. Also, I could not walk without someone helping me. I would persuade them that I could eat fruit, bagels, sandwiches and things like that until I could remember how to cook again. I told myself I needed to get all the strength I could muster up, pull everything out of my mind that I could remember, and concentrate as hard as I could to get this accomplished. They would believe that I would be able to stay by myself and take my medication. After they were gone, my plan was to quit taking the medication. That way, I could die. I did not want to live as an invalid, and I believed that I had a choice of deciding whether to live like that or not, and I chose not to. However, this was not to be.

    Even though my family had to leave, they had already made plans to take care of me. Bill had said that he would take care of me after they were unable to. He had wanted to take care of me all along, but they thought that they could stay through the summer until they had to go home. Also, Bill was still working a full time job and trying to run my business, as well as raising his own two children by himself.

I thought I would rather go to a nursing home. I remembered what the nurse in the hospital had told me about not going to a nursing home, because I would die there. Now that was what I wanted to do. I did not want Bill to have to miss any work, and I did not want to have to be any trouble to him. So I figured if I could go to a nursing home, then I could pretend to take the medication there and still be able to die as I planned. Bill had a different idea; he decided that he would take care of me and that I was absolutely not going to go to a nursing home. It was then that I decided to have a serious talk with my family. I asked them all to gather around the table so that I could talk to them, all but Shawn and Bill, because I knew that they would get very angry with me.

When they were all gathered, I very plainly tried to ask them to let me die. In broken sentences, I asked them whose life it was, who should have the choice, and to let me die. They were devastated that I was requesting this of them, and they were trying to explain to me that I was going to get better. I kept trying to tell them, "I'm not getting better, and I don't want to live like this." I told them that I was the one inside my body and mind, not them. I asked them to point out the ways that I was getting better, but they could not come up with any. I think at that point, I just about broke their hearts. I think they were afraid to go home then and afraid of what I might do, so they called Bill over and told him what I had said. He in turn was shocked and devastated and he also tried to explain to me that I was going to get better. He could not come up with any improvement that he saw in me either.

He said to me "You know, they're taking care of you and then I'm going to take care of you and you are going to get better." Nothing they could say could convince me that I was going to get better, because I was so within myself that I couldn't see the big picture. I felt so drugged and I was so miserable and so unlike my normal self that I just simply couldn't understand what they were trying to tell me. I couldn't believe that anything would ever change.

One thing I learned that night was that you can't kill yourself by holding your breath. I decided that they were not going to let me go in peace. They were going to make the decision that should have been mine, they were trying to keep me around because they wanted me around and I loved them for that, but I felt it should have been my decision alone. They could not see it from my point of view and just let me go. So, I tried to hold my breath, and I think I did pass out, but of course I immediately started breathing again.

It was at that point that I turned to God. I'd always believed in God, and I'd gone to church for most of my life, but I'd always tried to handle everything myself. I did know for sure that God had protected me, my mother, sisters and brother from being killed by my father when he was drunk and abusive. I knew that God had seen to it that I was aware that foster homes existed and had been given the choice to go into one to get away from my father. I was the oldest child and I was trying to fight him back when he was abusive; which put me in a more dangerous position than my brother and sisters. When I went out on my own at eighteen, and lived in a dangerous area, God protected me, of that I am certain. I did not have a car so I would have to walk through the city very early in the morning and late at night to get to the bus that took me to and from my college classes. Many people were robbed or attacked, but it never did happen to me. When

I was married, it seemed that I was unable to have children but after giving it up to God and praying about it, I was able to conceive and have my son. Throughout my life, I had made some bad decisions and put myself in harm's way, but I felt that God had always taken care of me. I always felt that God had assigned a guardian angel to look out for me.

I remembered very vaguely that brief moment before I went into the coma that I had prayed and asked God to please let me live long enough to raise my son. I decided to talk to God again about it, because he did let me live, but this was not living, and I would never be able to take care of Shawn in the shape I was in. So I prayed to God and told him that I appreciated that he had let me live and I appreciated that I had gotten the transplant. I truly did. But what good was it if I couldn't raise my son? I pleaded with God again that all I was asking for was to raise my son. I explained to God that I was so weak, I couldn't think clearly, I couldn't walk, could not cook or feed myself, and could not figure out how to take medication. How in the world am I ever going to take care of my son, when I could not take care of myself.

The thing that made me feel the saddest was that Shawn was helping take care of me, and he was only fourteen years old. He would sleep on the sofa at night in the room that they had put a bed in for me and would tell me what I was supposed to be doing no matter how many times I would ask him during the night. I prayed to God and said, "Please, please help me, because obviously I'm meant to live because every which way I've decided to die has not worked out for me. So please, please help me get better. Please help me get better so that I can raise my son. Please don't make Shawn's life miserable like I am right now by not having his mother be the same as she used to be, so please help me God."

In the next few days, I started to feel a little better physically. I could stand up and take a few steps with a walker. It was so amazing to me. I just couldn't believe it. I was so ecstatic that I was not totally exhausted all the time. I was actually able to sleep a couple of hours at a time. I knew that it would be one and a half weeks until Bill would be taking care of me and I wanted to be stronger before that time, because he would be trying to do the same thing by himself that my mom and my two sisters had been doing together.

I knew that this improvement was due to prayer and my family's love for me. Obviously God was helping me. Physically I was starting to feel a little better each day, but mentally I still couldn't think clearly most of the time. Mentally, I felt absolutely miserable. I was still hallucinating, and seeing and talking to people who weren't there, but I did not let my family know. At times, I still believed that the hospital was going to take the organ away from me if I did not get much better than what I was. I hated it when I had to go to the hospital to have my blood tested, for fear of what the results would be.

Eventually, I was able to get up and walk around my living room by holding onto things, but I could not go up the stairway. I was limited in how much walking I could do because my mind would stop me. Mentally, at a certain point, I just couldn't figure out what I was doing anymore and would have to go and lie back down. When my sister would help me exercise my arms and legs, it actually did not hurt as much as it always did before. I was getting really excited about the physical aspect. Mentally I wasn't improving at all, but I was still grateful that God was answering my prayers for physical improvement. I could not give credit to anyone but God for me getting better because nothing had changed drastically in my treatment plan at that point.

During that week and a half period of time, Bill would come to my house and my family would show him how to check blood sugar and how to give a shot if he had to, how to take my temperature, how to weigh me and what to look out for as possible signs of organ rejection. Bill didn't usually cook very much so they had to show him what my diet was supposed to be, and just generally tell him how to cook it. I was so concerned that he wouldn't be able to do all this. I just couldn't, in my mind, figure out how he could go from not cooking very many different foods to cooking special foods and how he could manage my medical regime. I could not figure out how he was going to work at his job too, and who was going to be with me when he was at work. He assured me that it was okay, that he was not going to be working during the time that he was taking care of me. That really bothered me because I knew my sister had lost her job already by being gone for a month taking care of me, and he was actually working in the job that he had always wanted, and I was so hoping that he wasn't going to lose his job too.

Chapter 18

IT WAS A BIG TRANSITION GOING FROM MY HOUSE TO MY FIANCÉ'S house. When we left my house to go to Bill's, my family was all in tears and crying. I looked at their faces, and I realized then that they didn't think I was going to survive. They had tried their best, and they were turning me over to Bill. He was just one person when the three of them really didn't feel that they had made much progress toward getting me better. They saw I had gotten stronger physically, but that had just been recent and they knew I might regress.

The biggest transition for me was that there was no bedroom at Bill's house for Shawn, and he would have to switch schools if he came to Bill's. He was going to stay with my ex-boyfriend. He lived right behind the high school where Shawn was starting and he could just walk to school. It was hard for me because I didn't want to be away from my son and I knew he did not want to be away from me. I wanted to be around him. I had gotten used to him being there at night in the same room with me. I was so afraid that I would never see him again. I thought that I might not survive after going to Bill's. Maybe by that time Shawn might not have come to see me, and I would never see him again.

I was really impressed by the way Bill was able to take care of me. He was able to cook, which just totally amazed me. He actually made everything on my diet, and he was able to check my blood sugar, my temperature, weigh me, and do all the things that the three of them had done. I realized that physically I was better when he started taking care of me than when my family was taking care of me because everything they had done for me was showing up in improvements that I could see. Therefore, it wasn't as hard to help me up and to help me get around. I just tired very, very quickly and couldn't stay up very long.

About a week after I'd been at Bill's, the telephone rang, and I could tell by his face that something wasn't right. He said to me, "We have to get to the hospital immediately." I asked him. "Why?" and he said, "Because you're having a rejection." "A rejection?" I asked him, "What are you talking about?" And he said, "Well, there's a problem with your liver and we have to get you to the hospital immediately." "It's happening," I told myself. "This is how I'm going to die. My body will reject it, and, as I understand it, it was so hard to get that organ in the first place, I'll never get another one. So this is how it's going to happen." I could tell by Bill's face that he was petrified too. I knew then that this was very, very serious. However, he said that the hospital had told him not to get excited, not to drive fast, but just to get me there as soon as he could and to bring a bag with my things in it because they were going to admit me.

When we arrived at the hospital and I was admitted, they told Bill and me that they were going to take me into a surgical room. They had to do a biopsy on my liver. I panicked at that. I thought they were going to cut me open. I thought they were going to put me under. I didn't want to be anesthetized, because I was so afraid I would slip back into a coma again. They told me that, no, I would not be put under, and that actually I would not need to be anesthetized. They said it was a very fast procedure, and they showed me something that looked like a big ink pen with the end of it like a clicker that clicks the pen open and shut. They told that they were simply going to hold it over the area where my liver was and that they were going to click it and it would go in my body and come out immediately with a little piece of my liver. They would be able to analyze it and tell us how bad the rejection was.

They took me into the surgical room, and performed the procedure on me, and afterwards they told me that I had to lie there for four hours and not move. This was something new for me. Perhaps this had happened in the hospital before they released me to go home, but if it had, I couldn't remember it. Perhaps it was happening all those times that I was so psychotic and didn't know who I was and where I was. I wondered how many other possible rejections that I had.

By the time the four hours were over, the results were back, and they knew I was having a rejection episode. They told me that they would be putting me into a room, and I would be there for three or four days, and that they were going to have to run a medication through me that was similar to the ones that I was currently taking, but much stronger. I thought to myself at that point, "I can barely think now. I can't imagine what it's going to be like to have a stronger medication going through my system." They assured me that it would only be for three or four days and that it would stop the rejection and for me to have faith in them and just to try to relax and get some sleep and some rest. At that time I was only averaging three or four hours at night and maybe three or four hours in the afternoon, and so I was really surprised at the hospital when the medication did actually almost knock me out to where I don't even remember being there much at all. After three or four days, I was okay to go home.

When I asked the hospital if this was normal, for the liver to try to reject, they told me yes, that it happens in almost every transplant patient. They did not know if it had happened while I was in the hospital right after my transplant or not. They told me that it usually happens within the first six months after the transplant, so not to be too concerned, that it wasn't an abnormal thing. I believed them, until two weeks later, it happened again. I was still having my blood tested every week. Again it was the same thing, Bill received a phone call and again I could see something was wrong by the look on his face. He looked at me and he said, "We have to go back again." He seemed to take it better than me. He said, "You know, they helped you last time. They stopped the rejection. It worked. I'm sure it'll work again this time."

He took me back to the hospital and I went through the same procedure again with the biopsy. I kept wondering how many pieces of the liver could be taken out by biopsy before there would not be enough of the liver left to function on. I had to lie still for four hours again and afterwards they admitted me. I was there again for four days having the medication run through an IV. I wasn't really upset about it this time, because I remembered last time that I had slept for most of the four days, and although I was skeptical, I did realize that I had very good doctors and nurses who did know what they were doing. I wouldn't have survived this long were it not due in a great part to them. I basically slept again for the four days, and I was really glad to go home. Right before I left the hospital, the nurse said to me, "Well hopefully we won't see you for a long, long time, because this has been two rejections in just a couple of weeks." I thought, *Yes, that would be great, if I didn't have to come back here for a long, long time.*

Unfortunately, that was not how it was to be. We'd been home for just couple of hours after leaving the hospital when they called again and said that they had taken blood right before I was discharged and they now had the results back. The blood showed that the rejection episode was not over or that I was having another separate rejection and I had to come back to the hospital immediately. With that, Bill argued with them, and said, "Maybe you're looking at the blood work from yesterday or maybe you're looking at blood work from a few days ago. How could that be? How can you discharge someone and get their hopes up that they're not going to be coming back for a while and make us turn around and come right back to the hospital?"

They told him it was urgent for him to bring me back there, because rejection episodes are very dangerous. All the way to the hospital I kept saying to Bill, "See I'm not getting better. I'm not going to get better. How could it be trying to reject so many times in such a short period of time." To me that seemed like an indication that now I was going to reject it once and for all. It was like being in a nightmare and not being able to wake up again. It was like being in the coma and trying to get out of it.

Bill told me to hang in there; that we would get through it, and that I would get better, and that he wasn't going to give up, and that he wasn't going to let me give up. I was pretty depressed at that point. Luckily, I only had to be in the hospital for a couple of days that time. After that, when I was released and I went home, every time the phone would ring, I would be so paranoid thinking that it was going to be the hospital calling again.

Chapter 19

THEY DID NOT CALL IMMEDIATELY, BUT DID CALL FOUR DAYS later. When the phone rang and I realized who Bill was talking to, I just wanted to starting screaming and not stop. I did not want to go back to the hospital again. They did not want me to go to the hospital for another rejection episode; it was far something worse. They said that I had contracted a virus, called a CMV (cytomegalovirus). It's a common virus that causes severe illness in transplant patients and people with compromised immune systems. They said for at least eight weeks I was going to have to have an IV every morning and every night for one and a half hours each time. I immediately thought that they meant for eight weeks I was going to have to be in the hospital.

They explained that they could have all the equipment delivered to the house and a home nurse could come by and train Bill to give me the IV himself. I would have to come to the hospital and have a "PICC line" (Peripherally Inserted Central Catheter) put into a vein in my arm for the IV to hook up to. The nurse said that we had to be very careful, and make sure that no air bubbles went into the line because they could go to my heart and cause a heart attack. The nurse would be coming by every two or three days to check on me would be able to help us if Bill needed any help or had any more questions or anything seemed to be going wrong. Bill hung up and told me that we needed to get ready to go to the hospital. When I hesitated, he told me if we did not get it under control, that I would definitely have another rejection problem.

With that, I asked him if he could call the nurse back so I could talk to her. Even though I wasn't able to really talk extensively, I was able to make myself clear when I asked her if it was going to be like this forever; if for the rest of my life that I was going to have to deal with one thing after another like this. I wanted to know if I was ever, ever going to get back to a normal life. I said to the nurse that I was told at the hospital that I could go back to a normal life and that I understood that it probably was not going to be *my* normal life, but *a* normal life. I did not think this constituted a normal life, going in and out of the hospital all the time, and having to have IVs run on me for eight weeks at a time in order to get rid of viruses.

What happened next was one of the most earth-shattering experiences that I have ever had — including trying to come out of the coma. The nurse, at the time, thought she was being positive and she thought that she was giving me something to feel good about and giving me something to keep me going. She said to me, "Look, you've gotten through the transplant. You survived it. You were lucky to get a transplant in the first place. Many people die waiting. Just think, with this transplant, you'll be able to live at least twelve years."

All I could say was "What, what are you talking about" over and over again. That was such a shock to me. At the time I was only forty-two years old. I could not imagine only living twelve more years. I had gotten to the point where I was feeling better. I was able to think a little more clearly. I was able to walk by myself. I had just gotten to the point that I could see that little glimmer of light at the end of the tunnel and was convincing myself that I could get there. Now they were telling me that I only had twelve years to live. When they had said that I could get back to a normal life, I just assumed that it would be the normal life like that of the rest of my family; they lived to be eighty or ninety years old. When she told me that, I couldn't talk. All I remember is the phone falling out of my hand and me sinking to the floor. I could feel myself becoming hysterical and I could not stop it.

Bill came rushing over and asked me what had happened. When I told him that I only had twelve years to live, even if I quit having all these rejection episodes and got rid of the virus, he asked me what I was talking about. I told him what the nurse had said to me, and he said, "That can't be. No one told your family or me that. We all thought that it was a permanent solution for you; that once your body would accept it, and you would get better physically and mentally, that you would be okay. There has to be some mistake. Maybe she doesn't know what she's talking about."

I explained that this was the same nurse that we've been dealing with all along. She knew what she was talking about. Bill picked up the phone and the nurse was still there and he asked her exactly what she told me. He then asked why they did not tell him or my family that. He wanted to know even if it was true, why did they tell me, knowing how badly it would upset me, and how something like this could set me back emotionally. He told her that we had been making some progress and now I was devastated. She explained that she had no idea that I did not know and was reminding me as a way to get me inspired to make it through these negative medical problems. She meant well, and I now realize that the timing was just bad.

After that, I sank into a major bout of depression. I basically did everything that Bill and the hospital staff asked me to do. I went along with eating, taking medication, walking around the house and trying to exercise some, but I didn't do anything extra. When he wasn't running the IV into me or if I didn't have to be to be up for eating or something, I just stayed in bed all the time. I just couldn't cope. I knew I was feeling sorry for myself, but I couldn't talk myself out of feeling that way. Finally, I was able to sleep whenever I wanted to. It seems like all I could do was sleep. At times, I didn't want to wake up; I just wanted to keep on sleeping.

As the days progressed, and I was having the IV run in me every morning and every night, I started getting to the point again where I couldn't think clearly. I could not think very clearly before this, but now it was even worse. Bill thought I didn't want to talk. But even when I did want to talk, I couldn't manage to say a sentence. It was like I was regressing back to where I had been weeks and weeks ago. The medication really had a grip on me, but instinctively I knew that it was getting rid of the virus.

One of the reasons that I was so depressed was that I wanted to see Shawn, but because of the virus, they really did not want me to be around other people unless I absolutely had to, so I wasn't able to see him. I really missed him. Additionally, no one else could come and see me either. My family had wanted to come to see me for a weekend, but they couldn't. The nurse who came in every few days wore a mask when she was there.

Finally one night I got to the point where I was desperate enough to plead to God for help again. I prayed to God everyday when I wasn't in a major cloud of depression and thanked him for being alive, but since he had helped me to improve somewhat physically, I didn't think

I should ask for anything else. I explained to God that I appreciated him helping me get back some of my strength in my body and I appreciated the transplant, but what use was it to have a physical body when I didn't have my mind. If I didn't have my mind, how could I tell my body what to do. I pleaded with God to help me, so I could get back to my son. I just wanted to raise my son, that's all I wanted in life at that time. I explained to God that after I was done raising him, I would be ok to go... to die... to whatever he chose for me. All I wanted was to get my mind back. After saying that prayer, I went to sleep. I was extremely tired. I wasn't able to really walk around the house anymore, to get any exercise, couldn't really do much of anything for myself; sleep was a great escape.

What happened the next morning was nothing short of amazing and in fact a true miracle. When I woke up, I felt fine. I had forgotten that I'd had a transplant. I had forgotten that I was ill. I had forgotten that I couldn't walk. It was the most amazing thing. I woke up and said to myself, "Wow, I'm hungry. I should make some breakfast." It was really early in the morning and Bill was out in the yard, doing yard work. I thought to myself, "I'll make him breakfast, and then I'll call him to come in and eat."

I took some eggs, bread and breakfast sausage out of the refrigerator. I looked at the clock and it was 8:00 a.m. I took the sausage and I put it on a plate and I put it in the microwave and I started feeling really tired and I was trying to think why I would be so tired. The thought occurred to me that maybe I was out late the night before, but I could not remember what I had done. I thought it strange that I could not remember. I was so tired that I decided to just sit down for a while. I sat down at the table and turned on the TV, and I was watching TV for a while and then I woke up with my head on the table. I felt better so I thought I should start making the eggs. I got up and I got a pan out and I started feeling tired again. I was thinking that maybe I was coming down with the flu, but in the middle of summer? That would definitely be unusual. I sat back down again for a while and eventually after getting up and down many times, I managed to make scrambled eggs, sausage and toast. I looked at the clock and it was 10:00am. I thought to myself that it had taken two whole hours just to make breakfast. I then opened up the back door, and yelled for Bill. He looked surprised when he saw me. He dropped his rake and came running up to the house.

He said to me, "What are you doing?" I told him I was making breakfast. He said "You're talking." And I said "Well, why wouldn't I be talking?" Then he said "What's wrong with you — you shouldn't be up and walking around by yourself, you could fall down." I asked him who I was supposed to be walking around with and why would I fall down. He was really making me angry because he was acting really strange. I thought for a second that I might be dreaming this, but realized I wasn't when he took me by the arm and was trying to get me to go into his living room and lie down on the sofa.

I told him to quit trying to get me to lie down and for him to eat breakfast. He turned around and looked in the kitchen and asked me if I had actually used the stove. When I explained that I had made eggs on the stove, he said that he was glad that I had not burned the house down. I was starting to get frustrated with the way he was acting. I thought he should be appreciative that I had made breakfast for him and I told him so. He looked at me and said, "Well, I don't understand." And I said, "I don't get what you don't understand." We stood there just looking at each other in confusion.

Then I said to him, "Well, why don't you wash your hands and eat breakfast, because I think it's already cold." He said, "Okay," and went to wash his hands. He came back to the kitchen and we sat down and ate breakfast. Everything was cold, but he did not say anything, he just continued eating. After we finished eating, he said that I needed to sit down because he needed to talk to me. I had no idea what he wanted to talk to me about, but I sat down.

He then asked me if I had seen or talked to someone at his house, just like I thought I had seen the nurse at my house — the one who did not exist and who told me that I did not have a liver transplant. I told him that I had not seen or talked to anyone. I couldn't figure out what he meant by that. He asked me if I remembered what had happened to me and what I was doing at his house. When he said that, I knew there was something important that I needed to remember, but I could not quite grasp what it was.

I told him then that he just needed to tell me what he had to say. He then said really slowly to me, "We have to give you your IV now. Do you remember that you're having IVs every day? In the morning and the evening? Remember the transplant?" Then, I remembered. I remembered the transplant. I remembered my mom and my sisters taking care of me. I knew everything, but it did not detract from the fact that I was thinking more clearly. I did not suddenly feel worse. I was still tired, but I still felt great compared to what I had been feeling. Then I understood why he had been so amazed at seeing me standing there. I had overnight gone from barely being able to talk or walk to getting up and making breakfast. True, it had taken me two hours, but I did get it done.

I told him that I knew why I was different that day than the day before. I told him that I had prayed last night and asked God to give me my mind back so that I could think more clearly because without my mind it didn't matter what my body was like, because the mind tells the body what to do. I told him that God had performed another miracle. That was three so far. First he enabled me to get a liver transplant when there were no organs available, then he helped my body get better, and now he was helping my mind get better. I told him that it was only up from there. I told him that I knew everything was going to get better. Bill agreed but he didn't want me to think that it was going to be that easy because so far it had been going from bad to good to bad again. It was just up and down and I knew that it was not going to be easy, but he just didn't know how much better I felt. He just didn't know how clearly I finally knew what was happening. He said that he could see a glimmer of what I used to be, the fighter in me. He said that he could see in me that strong-willed, knows-what-she-wants-to-accomplish, person that he had always known.

After breakfast, Bill gave me the IV and then I did start getting tired again so I wanted to lie down. After only lying down for a couple of hours, I wanted a snack and I wanted to wash my face and take a shower. It was different that I wanted to eat since I rarely wanted to because I had to eat so many times a day. Bill said he was concerned because he said that I only went in the bathroom when he took me and that I wouldn't look in the mirror because I told him that I could not see myself there. He said that I told him all I saw was a stranger looking back at me from the mirror. He said I also would not look at my body. He said he had encouraged me to look so that I could see that I was healing, but that I had refused and he did not want to argue with me. He said he was telling me that just in case I had forgotten because I did look different and he did not want me to be upset. He said that I could not take a shower because of all the tubes that were running into my body at various places, the cut from the transplant, and the PICC in my arm. He said I would have to wash off in the sink. He asked me if I wanted him to go into the bathroom with me. I told him that I needed to think about it.

I wasn't sure I was ready to see myself, so I lay there and thought about it for a little while. I decided I had to get it over with. I had to face it, because it must be horrible if I had argued with him about it. I told him that I was going to check it out and I would prefer to do it alone. I did not want him to see my reaction because I had no clue what my reaction would be, but if it was going to be bad, then I wanted to face it by myself. I wanted to see what I was going to have to change to get back to the way I used to look.

I took my clothes off, but I didn't want to look in the mirror yet. When I did look in the mirror, I looked down and I could see this huge, huge cut in me. I was cut all the way down my chest and all the way across my abdomen. I could see where there must have been big staples in me because there were actually holes on each side of the scar where the staples had gone in. I vaguely remembered when my family was taking care of me, being taken to the hospital and having those staples pulled out. I remembered it because I did not know they were going to take them out that day and it really hurt badly when they did.

I then looked down at myself and realized that I couldn't see my feet, and I thought to myself, "My God, what's wrong with me?" I wondered if I was pregnant and had forgotten about that also. I called to Bill and asked if there was something else that he had forgotten to tell me and when I asked him if I was pregnant, he got a good laugh at that. It was good to hear him laugh because I could not remember hearing him laugh or seeing him smile since my transplant. He was always very serious-looking when he was taking care of me. He explained that my abdomen was very swollen up, not just from where my scar was, but my entire abdomen. He said that I had lost my muscle tissue and the hospital wanted me to gain weight in preparation to doing some light exercises to get some muscles back and so I had gained at least 20 pounds. I then decided that I just needed to see a little bit at a time, just handle a little bit at a time, otherwise I would just be overwhelmed and it would slow down my recovery.

I put my housecoat back on. I looked in the mirror at my face and head then and what I saw in the mirror was very discouraging, because one side of my head had short hair and the other side of my head had really long hair. I then remembered them telling me that they'd had to shave part of my head whenever they had done surgery on my head. I look and I can see a big indentation in my head, just right above my forehead. I thought, "That must be where they cut me open and where they put the tubes in to release the ammonia." The hair was starting to grow over it, but the hair was so short that it was sticking straight up in the air. I thought to myself, "How can I cover that? What can I do?"

When I looked at my face in the mirror, I realized that my face was really, really round, and really, really big. I couldn't figure out what that was all about either. I decided to ask Bill, but I decided first to try to put on some makeup to see if that would help me to look more like myself. I couldn't remember the last time I had put makeup on. When I put the makeup on, it did make my eyes and mouth look better, but my face was so big. When

I came out of the bathroom, Bill was sitting there waiting for me.

He wanted to know if I was upset. I was but didn't want to discuss it with him. I was really embarrassed about how I looked. I just could not handle discussing my body at that time, but I needed to know why my face was so big. He told me that it was called 'moon face' by the doctors and nurses, and one of the drugs caused it. He said it caused me to retain water, but I had to take it because it was one of my anti-rejection drugs. He said that maybe, eventually, I would be able to be taken off of it, but for now, I had to take it.

He told me that the make-up looked good, but that I looked fine without it and shouldn't be using up my energy to put it on. I told him that it made my face look less swollen and he assured me that the swelling would eventually go down and back to normal. I did not know what to do about my hair with one side of it being really long and the other side of it really short. And he said, "Wait a minute." When he came back, he had some bandanas. He said, "Here, just tie the bandana over your hair and tie it behind. It's summer. It'll look like that's what you want to look like, and no one will need to know the difference. He said that I could get all of my hair cut off really short so it would all look the same. I didn't want to get my hair cut off short, for I had always had long hair.

After dinner and after Bill gave me the IV, I got up enough courage to discuss my body. He said after I got the muscle tissue back, then I could lose the additional weight. He said that was the plan. He said that I was mostly bones with skin hanging off of them when I was released from the hospital. I decided right then and there that every day I was going to walk around the house as much as I could. I asked Bill if he could get my scales from my house, and that way, every day, I could see how I was doing. I still wasn't ready to go outside. For some reason, I was afraid to go outside. I only felt safe in the house.

The next morning the nurse came to clean and re-bandage all the places on my body that needed to be taken care of. She was astonished when she saw me up and walking around. Before that I had always been lying down or sitting in a chair. She told me she had been so concerned that I wasn't making any progress, and she was amazed at how well I was doing. I then asked her if she could get me a list of exercises that I could be doing and if I could use any weights yet. She said I couldn't use any weights, but I definitely could do some exercising. She said she would bring them back next time she came, so that I could get started on an exercise regime to get my strength back.

She told me that, in the meantime, until I saw her again, that I needed to just keep walking as much as I could, but to also try to go outside, because I needed to get some air. She said she was aware that I had practically been indoors for two and a half months since being in the hospital except for the times I was taken to doctors' appointments, taken to the lab to have blood work done and transferred from my home to my fiancé's home.

After that, my continual prayer to God was to please not let me relapse. I did not want to go backwards. I just wanted to keep making steady progress. I was tired of being depressed. Even though I had some pretty bad things happen in my life, I had never gone through periods of depression until all this had happened. I was a strong person and could probably handle anything that I would know was going to happen, such as a grandparent dying, but this entire situation had blindsided me. I also prayed that I could start remembering things better, just over all be able to use my mind to a greater capacity.

I thought continuously about seeing Shawn. I knew that I could not see him or anyone until after the IV was run through me for the eight weeks and I had been tested and cleared that the virus was gone. I was also entertaining the idea of going home after the virus was gone. I decided to talk to the hospital about it the next time I went there for a checkup. The next time that I went in for a checkup, I wasn't in a wheelchair. I walked in. They were very surprised and could not believe the way that I looked, especially since I was dealing with a virus. They had never seen me with make-up on. They had only seen what I looked like when I was dying from liver failure, and when I was trying to survive after the transplant. I had been in a wheelchair at the last appointment and I had told them I knew I was not going to survive. At the time I was very serious, so my attitude at this appointment was startling for them to see.

One of the nurses asked to what I attributed this change, and I explained to her that I had prayed to God and I asked for my mind back and that somehow he had given it back. She said that she had seen many miracles in all the years that she had been a nurse and that in my case he was definitely a strong God to have given my mind back through all the medications that I was on. She said some of the side effects of a couple of medications were that they were mind-altering and could subdue you to the point where you couldn't think clearly.

So now I knew why sometimes I couldn't say a whole sentence. I asked the transplant doctor if I could go home after all the IVs were run through me. I told him that I realized I couldn't run an IV on myself, but if it got rid of the virus, then I could take care of myself. I also told him that I had a positive attitude now and could be trusted to be by myself. Since the time at my house when my sister told the transplant nurses that I wanted them to just let me die, I was not supposed to be alone. He told me to not get my hopes up, because it was going to take a long time for me to get my strength back. He said that no matter how positive my mind was my body still had to get better before I could take care of myself.

He said the number one thing they looked for when allowing someone to be home alone was that they could take their own medication. He said I had to be able to totally take care of myself before he sent me home. He said the nurse could only come once a week when I went home, whereas right now, the nurse was coming three times a week. He told me to just deal with one thing at a time. He said we needed to get through running the IVs for the eight weeks and then we could discuss further about me going home.

I decided right then and there that he was wrong. I knew I would be able to go home soon after the IVs; somehow I just knew it. I would be with my son sooner than anyone thought. I didn't care what I had to do or go through to get home, because I would do it. Then Shawn and I could start to get our lives more back to normal, back to the way it was before. That was my goal and ambition. I had always believed in living life to the fullest and not wasting a minute of it and I felt like a lot of my life was gone because of this illness and recovery and I could never get it back.

After about the fourth week of the IVs for the virus, the hospital told me that perhaps I might not have to have the IV treatment for the full eight weeks. They said they usually run it the entire course to be sure that it was gone, but that my blood work was looking so good that it might not be necessary. They said that we could try to cut it down to six weeks. I realized then that I only had two weeks to convince Bill and the nurses and doctors that I was at the point of taking care of myself. I made an appointment at that time to go back in two weeks. I told the transplant doctor that I wanted to discuss with him at that appointment about going home. He told me that I would probably not be ready to go home yet.

I asked him to tell me exactly what I needed to be able to do before I could go home, so the hospital gave me a list of things. Many of them I was already doing. I decided I was going to learn everything on the list, and if I couldn't, I would fake whatever it was. I realized at that point that one of the reasons that I hadn't gotten better faster was that I was so independent and that I hated being weak and needing someone to take care of me, so I fought the help. I still wanted to take care of myself. I wanted to be able to get back to where I had been before. The nurses had told me at the hospital that there would be limitations, so to take it slowly.

During the previous four weeks while I was getting the IV, I was progressively getting better, except I was so, so tired all the time. It was a combination of factors, including the medication, the IV, and my weakened overall physical condition. I did learn how to do my own medications, and I wouldn't let Bill give them to me any longer. I would set a timer, so that I wouldn't forget to take them. I proved to him repeatedly that I could manage, and he finally trusted my improving abilities, although he would still ask, just to be sure.

I asked him if I could try driving again. He told me that I could try driving in the driveway but only when he was at home. He sat in the car with me in the driveway, and I was slowly learning to drive again. I had to learn from scratch, because I really couldn't remember how to do it, and then once the car started moving, it scared me. Just the feel of the way that the car moved didn't seem familiar to me. That part of my memory didn't come back. At last he was able to go places and not have to be home with me all the time. He asked me not to drive when he was not there, but I would find his keys and drive his car up and down the driveway until I felt comfortable with what I was doing. Eventually he did let me drive around the area with him in the passenger seat. He was amazed at how well I was doing, because he had no clue that I had been going up and down the driveway without him when he wasn't at home.

My friends had been calling Bill all the time and asking how I was doing. I didn't want to see them, because I didn't want them to see the way I looked. Now that I could think clearly and I could talk, I thought they would never let me go home if I was afraid to go anywhere other than the driveway. I knew that I must appear to be much better even though I was extremely tired. When one of my friends called and offered to come over and take me someplace, I readily agreed. Bill was really shocked because I would not let him take me out any place except to practice driving; but he was happy that I was going with somebody. My friend offered to take me to a card shop, where I could get cards to send to everyone to thank them for all the support and all the prayer and everything they had done for my family and me.

When she came over, I was worried that I would not be able to pull it off, because I was so tired that day, but I knew I had to try. She helped me get into her SUV, and she took me to a store, and I was able to walk around and find a number of cards. When I started feeling tired, I did not let her see it. I didn't want her to tell Bill that I'd gotten out and couldn't stand up or didn't have enough energy to be there very long; so I pretended that everything was okay. That was difficult at times, because I had to hold onto the card racks when I felt like I was going to pass out. When we arrived back at Bill's house, my friend told him that I did fine. He was surprised because we had been gone for two hours and he thought that maybe I had gotten sick while we were out, but my friend assured him that I hadn't.

Everything was improving except for the tiredness. My mind was still the same. I was able to take my medication by myself and walk around the house and actually make a lot of the meals. Because of this, Bill could actually take out more time between the morning and the evening IVs to do other things. He could go visit friends. He could just do more. He wouldn't go back to work at this point because he was afraid I would have a relapse. I told him I was fine but he wouldn't go back to work until I was able to go home. That gave me even more incentive to go back home, because I knew that he had given up the best job that he had ever had in order to take care of me. He couldn't get a family medical leave to take care of me, because we weren't married and I wasn't family. I knew he had quit his job. I had overheard his mother talking to someone about it on the phone when she was at his house.

During the day then, I would do the minimal amount of things I had to do when he was gone. I would lie down and rest quite a bit. When he was at home, I could pretend like I was feeling great, whether I was or not. I could take my medication, I would walk when he was at home, and I would exercise. The nurse had brought me a one-pound weight and was giving me different exercises to do with my hands and arms. When he was at home, it appeared to him that I was getting so much better. I was getting better in other ways than physically. I was really remembering more and was able to do many things, but the tiredness was still debilitating. I was able to cook practically every day, and that made it seem even more that I was getting back to normal. Ever since the day that I was able to make breakfast, I had been calling my family and telling them how much better I was getting. At first, there was total silence on the other end of the line and then my sister asked to speak to Bill. When he confirmed my improvement, they were delighted just to hear that I was getting up, but they were still skeptical.

I knew then that they had had the same fear that I was not going to survive. I remembered the look on their faces when I was leaving my house to go to Bill's house. They were afraid that they were going back to West Virginia and that they were never going to see me again. Then when they decided to visit for a weekend and give Bill a break, they couldn't because I had the virus and was having the IVs and was contagious. I had been trying to call them at least every few days, because I wanted to get them on my side concerning going home. I wanted them to agree with me that I was able to go home at the end of the two weeks after the IV was finished.

Two weeks had gone by, and it was time for my doctor's appointment. I had everybody convinced that I was okay to go home. Bill didn't really want me to go, because he was the only one that suspected that I wasn't quite ready. However, I was prepared. When I went into the doctor's office, I had my list in my hand that they had given me telling me all those things I needed to be able to do before I could go home. I showed them everything I could do. I could cook, I could shower, and I could take my own medication. There wasn't anything on the list that I couldn't do, so the doctors agreed to let me go home. They said they would have a nurse come by once or twice a week at first. They taught me how to change my own bandages and dressings, so that I could do them myself on the days when the nurse or Bill couldn't come over. I assured them that my son was fourteen and he would be able to help me also.

Ever since I started feeling better again and was able to take care of myself more, I started calling Shawn and telling him that we would both be home soon. I told him that it would just be a matter of weeks, but I don't think he believed me at first. He was so excited when I called him and told him what day I would be there. Both of us could not wait to get back to our own home. I was grateful for Bill, my mother and sisters and for the hospital staff and everything that everyone had done for me, but I really wanted to get back to my own place with my son. It was one step closer to getting back to a life, any life.

Chapter 20

THE DAY THAT I WENT HOME WAS EXTREMELY TIRING AND I found that I had to spend the first two or three days in bed all the time. I soon decided that I couldn't do that anymore when I saw the worried look on Shawn's face. He was really happy to be back in his own home, but I could tell that he was really concerned about whether I was getting better or not. I devised a plan to get up in the morning and get him off to school, then I would go back to bed, and stay in bed all day, until a few minutes before he came home. Then I would get up, get dressed and act like I'd been up all day long. I figured if he saw this, he wouldn't worry so much about me. I would then make him dinner and do whatever I needed to do around the house and then go to bed when he went to bed. He would never know. He would think that I was doing just fine.

After being home for a few days, I realized that I had forty-some messages on my answering machine. These were all messages that came in while I was at Bill's house, because Karen had returned the calls from when they were taking care of me. I was so overwhelmed by all the calls and all the people. Many were friends who were still offering to take me into their homes and take care of me and help me if I needed it. The sad part was, I didn't know who half of these people were. I could tell by the messages they were leaving that they knew me very well.

After a few weeks had gone by, I was still staying in bed all day until Shawn would get home, but I was out driving some in the evening, going to the grocery store and different places like that. Then a strange thing happened to me one morning. I got up as usual and got Shawn ready to go to school, and the next thing I knew, I found myself on the expressway driving to somewhere. I didn't realize what I was doing, and I didn't know where I was going or what my intentions were, so I pulled off to the side. I could not figure out what was happening, and, for a few minutes, couldn't remember who I was or what I was doing. Then the realization of what happened to me came back to me, and I got back on the expressway and turned around and went back to my home.

I would find many times in the evening, when I would get in my car to go someplace, I would drive a few blocks and I would have to stop, because I couldn't remember where I was going. I then got into the habit of taking a post-it note and writing on it exactly the places that I was going and putting it on my steering wheel. That way when those things happened to me, I could look at my note and continue on with the chores that I was going to do. I was very frustrated to have to do this, but it was a solution to deal with all the confusion.

One morning I actually got up, dressed in work clothes, and I had driven forty minutes and found myself in a parking lot of a company, before I realized what I was doing. I looked up and saw the name of the company on the building. I realized that this was the company where I worked. The problem was that I had no memory of getting dressed and getting ready and driving there. Again, I turned around and went back home.

My briefcase and my planner had been in my bedroom when I had arrived home the first day, but I hadn't looked at them yet. I decided to go through my briefcase, look at everything that was in it to see if I could remember anything. By looking through the briefcase and looking through the planner, I saw what I had been doing for the last six months before I became ill and what I was supposed to be doing in the next three months after I became ill. Very little of it made sense to me. I had vague memories of some people I worked with, and of the office where I worked, and I had vague memories of standing in front of people and training them. However, when I looked at all the information about a computer system that I had just purchased for the company before I became ill and all my drawings and detailed information about how I was going to install it during the three months after I became ill, none of it made sense to me. It was as if everything that I had ever learned was gone. I had traces in my memory, but not enough to even have a full picture of anything that I had done at my job.

I decided the way to confront this problem was to face it head on. I called the office where I worked at and talked to the receptionist and asked if it was all right to come in and see everyone. I didn't say that I didn't know who anyone was; I just said that I'd like to come in and see everyone. I asked her what would be a good day and a good time. She told me around 11:30 the next day would be good, because that was about the time that people went to lunch, and that she would tell everyone that I was coming in and probably everyone would just bring a lunch so they could stay there and talk to me. I thought that would be a good idea, because I felt sure that if I saw my office and saw the place where I worked and saw the people that I worked with that it would definitely trigger my memories. Sometimes my son or fiancé or family would say something to me, and it would trigger a memory. I felt sure that if I did go back to the company where

I worked, that everything would come back to me; everything that I had learned, everything that I knew, everything about computers. I thought I finally had a good plan in place to get the memory problem solved.

The next morning I called one of my friends who I did remember and who I knew had worked with me at the company. She was not currently working there, but I asked her how to get there. Although I'd gone there and found myself in the parking lot, I did not actually know how to get there. It was as if my mind had gone there automatically on that day. She gave me instructions, and she was pretty cool about it. She was one of my friends who had offered to take me into her home and take care of me. She was also the one who came to the hospital when I was in the coma and told them she was my sister in order to get in to see me. She didn't act surprised or anything. She didn't act like she couldn't believe that I didn't know how to get there. She just simply gave me the directions and told me to call her when I came back to let her know how it went.

I arrived at the building and went in through the front door. To the left was a small office, and to the right was an office that had many desks and a long hallway. As soon as I walked in the door, the receptionist jumped up and grabbed me and hugged me and told me she was so glad to see me again and asked me had I gotten all of her cards. She must have realized by the look on my face that I did not know who she was. I felt so bad. I thought it was not going so well if I could not remember the first person I saw. She was pretty good about it. She said she used to work in a nursing home, and she heard that I had memory problems and therefore she understood entirely.

She started to tell me some things about herself; how long she had worked there, how long we'd known each other. It hadn't been long, only been about six months, and she said probably because I'd been taking the medication for nine months, before it finally put me into a coma, it explained why I didn't remember her. She said not to worry about it, that she wasn't offended by it, and that she totally understood. I realized that I must have worked with some really nice people if she was an example.

At least thirty people were waiting for me in the lunchroom and many crowded around me. Some people's faces actually looked familiar to me, and some people I did not recognize at all. I was really feeling like a stranger in a place that Bill told me that I had worked at for twenty-two years. I had practically grown up there. I had started working there when I was twenty. I did recognize a man who was much, much older than I, and I remembered that he had been like a father to me, and that my son was named after him. I spent an hour there, most of the time nodding my head and smiling and hugging people and just pretending, because I had no clue who the majority of the people were, although they all definitely knew me. I didn't know who had come to the hospital. I didn't know who had brought clothes for my mother. I didn't know who had gotten the money together to give me. I didn't know who had paid for the hotel for my family to stay in the hospital. I didn't know who they all were, so I had written out a card thanking everyone, and I asked them to post it on the board, and I was able to thank them all there in person as well.

All I could do on the way home was cry and cry and cry. I was crying so much that I couldn't even see my directions and got lost twice trying to get home. When I arrived home, Shawn was there, and when he saw my face and saw how upset I was, he wanted to know what had happened to me. He thought I'd been at the hospital and they'd given me bad news. I explained to him that I had gone there, and I didn't know who most of the people were. He said, "Cheer up Mom, your memory will come back and then you'll know who they all are. Then you can go back there again and have a good time seeing everybody."

Shawn was always saying positive things to me like that, but today I could see the worry in his eyes. I think he realized how tired I was all the time. He may even have known that I'd been faking it and been in bed all the time during the day. I thought this because one day he said to me, "Mom, why do you get up with me for breakfast? I really don't want eggs. I really don't want a cooked breakfast. I really would just like to have some cereal. So mom, please stay in bed. Don't get up when I go to school. I'm in high school. I don't need you to get up and make breakfast for me. And I'll come upstairs and I'll kiss you goodbye, and that way you'll know I'm up and out and ready to go to school." Although I should have been glad to see my son being so responsible like that, it really made me feel sad that a fourteen-year-old had to be that adult at that age.

I thought, all in all, I had done a pretty good job of fooling a lot of people that I worked with into believing that I knew who they were, and I was glad that I had done that because I didn't want them to know the truth. I wanted them to know how grateful I was and how thankful I was and how happy I was to have known such nice people. A few days after I was there, I received a phone call from a guy who said, "Hey Annie, how are you doing?" I said to him, "I'm sorry, but, I think you have the wrong number." He said, "No, no, I for sure have the right number." I replied, "Well, my name's not Annie." He said, "Oh yeah it is, at least that is what I always called you." I said, "No, I really think you have the wrong number." His voice changed, "You really don't know who this is, do you?" Then he said, "You know, I wasn't here when you came by the other day, and some of the people thought that maybe you didn't know who some of them were either. I didn't realize that you had such a problem now with your memory."

I explained to him that I did have a memory problem and asked how I knew him. He told me that I definitely should know him, since twenty years ago he and I were engaged, and we lived together for two years. I felt so bad at that point and I apologized to him. I told him that maybe if I saw him, I would know him. I explained to him that I remembered sometimes by seeing someone and sometimes when they told me things about themselves to trigger my memory. He said that if being told that we were engaged did not trigger my memory, then nothing probably would. I did not want to hurt his feelings so I told him again that I was sorry and that I needed to go. He then said, "Let me tell you some different things about when we were together and about where we work." And I said, "How long did you work with me?" And he said, "I've worked with you for the whole twenty-two years that you've been there. I was already working there when you started." So he started telling me some different things about where he worked in the company, and actually I did have a vague memory concerning him, but not enough to really remember. I was just happy to have a slight memory, because I did not want to hurt his feelings. Once he started giving me other information, I could remember a little more.

The next time that I went to the hospital and talked to the transplant team, I told them about my memory problem; that I didn't recognize people whom I had known for many years. They told me that they needed to run some neurological tests, because they weren't sure what kind of memory problem I was having and whether it was from the coma or the stroke. They knew I had some memory loss since coming out of the coma, but they weren't sure of the extent. They would set me up for a number of tests to find out just what had happened and to see if there was something that they could do to correct it.

Even though I fought it very, very hard, I could feel myself sinking into a depression over the memory loss. The fact that I couldn't remember what I did at my job, and that I did not recognize most of the people there made me realize that I probably couldn't go back to work very soon, if ever. That really bothered me because all I wanted to do was get back to the life that I had in the past. According to my family and my friends, I had been such a happy person. I had really loved my life. I had loved my job. I had loved my friends. I had loved going to college. I loved my business. I had loved everything. Well, my business was now gone, and my job might be gone, and I couldn't remember a lot of my friends. I tried as hard as I could to resist, but I could still feel myself sinking and losing hope.

Chapter 21

Soon after that I discovered I was having other problems. One moment I would be walking along, and the next I would find myself on the floor. While driving, I would suddenly be about to run into the back of the vehicle in front of me. I would be speaking a sentence to someone, and then I couldn't finish it, because I couldn't remember what I had just said. I hated to go back to the hospital and tell them this, because it seemed as if all I had to tell them was negative. I was extremely appreciative to be alive and to have survived the coma, stroke and transplant and I wanted them to know that too. I knew that, for my own safety and in order to be able to take care of my son, I had to go to them and tell them how extreme my problems were becoming. They expedited setting up tests for me so they could find out what was happening.

After a number of tests had been run, and I had talked to numerous doctors and specialists, they came to the conclusion that I was having seizures. They thought the problems were caused either by the medication doing damage to my brain before it put me in the coma or by something had happened to me during the coma or the stroke. They ascertained that I had some permanent long-term memory loss and also that my short-term memory was very bad at that point in my life. They told me then that there was no way that I could go back to my job, especially since I couldn't remember what I had done there. I had admitted to them how bad it was in the hope that they could find a way to solve these problems, so I was shocked when they told me that my memory would probably never improve. They gave me a list of ways to try to retain memory. It was similar to the list that they give to Alzheimer patients or stroke victims. They also started me on yet another medication to control the seizures. I was glad to get the seizures stopped but I was beginning to realize that I would have a lot of side effects from all the medications that I had to take. I simply wanted to feel like I had before all this happened; when I did not ever take any medications.

I was absorbed in trying to pretend that I was okay in front of Shawn, and trying to control some of the side effects of the medications, and act like the memory problems didn't exist. I found myself just staying at home and not wanting to go out anywhere unless I absolutely had to. When Bill would want to come over, I would always have an excuse. I didn't want to tell him that I didn't want to see anyone at all. I didn't want to tell him I wanted to be completely alone in the house, with just my son there. After all he had done for me, I didn't want to hurt his feelings. And it really had nothing to do with him. It was only that I had all of these restrictions in my life now, and I was having such a hard time dealing with them and hiding it from everyone.

I had had such high hopes of being able to get back to my life, the life that I had before, or to a somewhat normal life. This was not a normal life. Not knowing the people around me, not knowing my friends that I had had for twenty-some years, not knowing a job that I had been doing for twenty-two years, not knowing anything about computers. I couldn't even fix my own computer. When something would go wrong with it, I would have to ask my son, and I had been a computer project manager. I had bought, installed and programmed computers and trained people how to use them; now, when my computer had the least little problem, I didn't have a clue as to what was wrong with it. It was devastating to me. However, I kept telling myself to be thankful that I was getting better physically and mentally I could think clearly. I was still grateful for that and thanked God for that everyday.

No matter how hard I tried to fight it, I knew that every day I was spending less and less time going outside and more and more time in the house, specifically in my room. That room was like a haven for me. Luckily Shawn was in his first year of high school, was involved with a lot of his friends, and into many activities after school. He didn't really notice how my mental attitude had deteriorated.

Bill, however, was persistent. When he came over to see me, he could see the change in me and he kept reminding me how lucky I was to be alive and how lucky I was to be able to think clearly again and that I was at home again and that I could start a new life. He kept repeating over and over again that it was better than the alternative, that I could have died. I wanted to say to him many times, "Easy for you to say that. You haven't had to start your life all over again. I can tell you like your life too. And how would you want to be starting all over again from scratch, not having a clue what you could do because of all the restrictions?" I knew I was feeling sorry for myself and I hated that. I had never felt sorry for myself since long ago when I was a child living in fear of my father.

Bill had asked me how my hands were feeling. I didn't even understand then what he was saying or why he was asking me that. I had been dropping many things, but I rationalized it as nervousness. He asked if my hands were numb. I realized then that I could barely feel my hands at all. He reminded me that this had been the beginning of my medical problems, when I developed carpal tunnel and had surgeries that hadn't worked. I had been sent to a rehabilitation center and a doctor had given me the drugs that had destroyed my liver. He told me that it was time to go back to my hand surgeon, to see if something could be done to improve my hands.

He pointed out that I really needed to understand what my limitations were so that I could have the entire recovery "picture." I needed know what areas were going to get better and what areas were permanently damaged. I didn't remember who my hand surgeon was and Bill didn't either, but he went through my wallet and he found a business card from that doctor. I made an appointment to see him. I called the receptionist at the office the morning of my appointment and asked for directions to get there. She said, "You've been here twenty, thirty times. You can't remember how to get here?" I explained to her that I had been ill and that I was a little foggy and just needed directions again, and she was very kind about it and gave me the best directions on how to get there.

When I came into the doctor's office, I signed in, but the receptionist was busy doing some typing, looking the other direction, so I sat back down again. Pretty soon the doctor opened the door and called my name out, and I looked up at him and he looked at me and looked beyond me and looked around and said to his receptionist, "Isn't Patricia here?" She said, "Yes, I think she must be out there because she signed the check-in book." I said to him, "Hi, I am right here." He couldn't believe it was me. He tried very hard to mask his surprise. It must have been the weight gain, the swollen roundness of my face and the bandana covering my shaved head. It might just have been the look on my face. Whatever it was, he hadn't recognized me.

He was, however, very professional and said, "Oh, oh, yes, okay, come on in." He tried to act very nonchalant, but when we got into his office, he said to me, "What has happened to you? I'm so sorry, but I need to be blunt with you. I don't even recognize you. I mean I know it's you, but you don't look like the same person. Your demeanor is different and you just look different. I'm used to seeing you walking in here in a suit with a briefcase and asking all kinds of questions. What has happened to you?"

I broke down hysterically at that point and told him every single thing that had happened to me. I was really embarrassed but just couldn't control myself. He couldn't believe it. When I mentioned the drug, he said that he had heard that drug had been taken off the market, but he didn't realize that it had killed so many people and that many people who did survive taking it had to have liver transplants. After we had gotten through all my drama, he then asked me how my hands were feeling. I told him that I could barely feel my hands at all. He said the stroke or coma might have done more damage to them, because I had been getting some feeling back in one of them.

He reminded me that I had been having physical therapy and occupational therapy on my hands before my illness. I flashed back to seeing the therapists at the hospital, and trying to not let them know it was me in the wheelchair when my family had taken me there to the lab for blood work. He said that although there was a lot of permanent damage to the hands before my transplant and some feeling that would never come back, the hand seemed much worse now.

He asked if he could test with pins to see how much feeling I did have. And I told him "yes," so he took a few pins and he stuck them in my fingers. Although I could feel the pressure of the pins, it was not painful. I could tell by the look on his face that he was really surprised at my loss of feeling. He explained that I must be very, very careful because my hands were so bad that I could burn or cut myself, I might drop things and break them around me, and I might not be able to feel the steering wheel when I was driving.

He talked to me for a long time about how we were going to accommodate the problem with my hands. I asked him if he thought as I grew stronger and got better and recovered from my illness, I might get some feeling back in my hands. He said he doubted it because they seemed so very bad. I thanked him for being so candid with me and telling me exactly what my chances of improvement were. I tried to get out of the building before I started crying again.

I was starting to get used to the tears. I was a person who never, ever, ever cried. It took so much to make me cry. The only times I really remember crying in my life were when someone very close to me died. Now, I found I couldn't control the tears, that every time anything the least bit negative happened to me, all I could do was cry. I told myself I had to pull myself together because I couldn't let my son see me like this and I didn't want it to affect him permanently.

Bill came over that night to hear what the doctor had to say. He said he wasn't really surprised at the fact that my hands were so bad, because he had noticed that when I ate I kept dropping my silverware, and that I had dropped many things at his house once I was up and walking around and broke many glasses and plates. I realized I had done that, but I just didn't realize how many that I had broken. But, as usual he was my cheerleader, along with my family, who would call me all the time and cheer me on, and tell me that I was going to get back to a normal life, to just keep on hanging in there, that, as always, they had faith in me and they knew how strong I was.

What they all didn't understand was that, unlike most people, I used to have a lot of control over my life, and for the first time since I was eighteen years old I felt that I had no control at all. I tried to be cheerful and carry on as if nothing was wrong, but finally Bill came to me and said, "Look, you need to see a therapist. Because you just... you're not getting any better... mentally, you're just sinking lower and lower." I got an attitude and told him "You know, I have a social work degree and a sociology degree and I've had many psychiatric and psychology classes and I don't need to talk to someone. I can handle this on my own." But Bill said to me, "No, you can't handle it on your own. You've tried and you can't handle it on your own. You really need to see someone. Why don't you just try, and then if you feel like it's not doing you any good, then don't go anymore." He said that there was a place that was close to where he lived that he had heard was very good and he had stopped by and gotten me a card.

I called to make an appointment, but they said first I had to see a psychiatrist and then I could see a therapist. I was really surprised at how nice the psychiatrist was. He spent a lot of time with me, and he let me explain to him everything that happened to me. Then he said, "Well, no wonder you're here. Nobody could withstand everything that you've been through, and not feel like they needed to talk to someone and get some help. Here, you can talk to someone. It never goes any place else. You can say whatever you want. You don't have to worry like you do about upsetting your son and your family and your fiancé. That's what we are here for. The therapist and I will be here for you to talk to and you don't have to be afraid to let your emotions out."

He said that it did not matter how I thought it would sound, because that is what I needed to do — to get my feelings out in the open and be aware of them for only then could I deal with them. He said they could help me come up with a solution on how to handle changes, since it appeared that I was not going to be able to go back to the life that I once had. He said, "Temporarily, we need to have a way in order to get your emotions controlled. I would recommend that you should try a low dose anti-depressant." I told him, "I'm already on so many medications. I had never taken any medication in my entire life before my transplant, and now I'm on all kinds." But he assured me, "Just take it for now. It'll help you feel better. After a while, after you see the therapist, maybe you'll be able to come off them. For right now, you need to be able to sleep. You need to be able to not worry all the time. You need to not feel that your life is so out of control." I agreed to try it, and I was really surprised a couple of weeks later when I did feel somewhat better. I did not feel like I was drugged. I did not feel fantastic, but I did not cry all the time, just occasionally. What the medication did was kind of even it out and help me feel calmer.

By that time I'd had one appointment with the therapist, and he was really great. He spent the first appointment just letting me talk and telling him everything that had happened to me, just like I had told the psychiatrist. And he set up his first sessions twice a week with me and then he said we would go down to once a week and then once every two weeks and then once a month and then as needed, until I felt like I would be able to handle everything on my own. He was very nice about it. He said that usually his clients came in with only one problem. But, he said, I was a patient with an array of problems because my business had been shut down and I probably would not be able to go back to my job and I was really restricted in what I could do. He said it might take a little longer than normal in my case to get my life back together.

He said even though I had many, many things going on in my life, he felt sure that, between us we could somehow work it out so I could get back to a life that I would be happy with. He said there are always many different ways of having a life; just because you were so happy with your life before does not mean that you cannot find a new life and be just as happy in that. I told him that my biggest struggle was not working, because I had been working since I was fourteen years old. He suggested that I talk to the transplant team of doctors and nurses at the hospital and see if there was anything that I could do there just for a few hours a week that would make me feel like I was doing something worthwhile.

Perhaps I could volunteer to work with transplant patients or visit transplant patients in the hospital and give them encouragement. I started having a friend go with me to the transplant floor in the hospital and I would ask the nurses if they had any transplant patients that might benefit from a visit. The first time I went there, I saw the nurse that had told me to never allow myself to be put in a nursing home because I would die there. She did not recognize me at all because I had started trying to do my hair and put makeup on and I had lost at least 10 pounds of the weight. Also, my face was not nearly as swollen up because the hospital had lowered the amount of the steroid that I had to take.

I also talked to the social workers at the hospital and was surprised to find out that on every other Wednesday afternoon a number of families came to the hospital because one of their loved ones was at the top of the transplant waiting list. The patient and family would watch the actual surgery on a film, and then discuss before and after treatment plans and the family's role in helping the transplant patient get better. Then for an hour after that they had a support group and patients like myself, who had survived a transplant, talked to the group and answered questions.

At first I was really reluctant, because I didn't want to be reminded of the transplant, even though I was reminded every day because I had to take the anti-rejection medication every twelve hours and various other medications in between. The next session I had with my therapist, I told him, "I don't know if I can handle it. Maybe I'll start crying. I don't want to start crying in front of the patients." And he said, "No, no, I don't think that you will. I think that you will see it will be a positive thing for you and for them. It will make you see how lucky you are, even with your limitations, because when see them you will see in them how very ill you really were, and you will realize that you are living and that you can make another life for yourself."

He must have done some research concerning transplants because he told me that some of the patients I would be talking to would not survive long enough to get a transplant and that would put my life in prospective. He was very encouraging, so I did start going and talking to these people who were waiting, and it really did help me. It allowed me to see that I could be of aid to someone. It actually gave me great satisfaction to encourage these people and to be able to give them answers that sometimes the nurses and doctors could not. The patients and their families really wanted to get information from the point of view of a transplant patient. It was very rewarding.

Chapter 22

ABOUT THIS TIME, I REALIZED THAT I WAS RUNNING SHORT OF money to pay my bills. This was how life was with me now; I didn't really consider anything until it happened, and then that's when I would attempt to handle it. I couldn't figure out what to do, because the doctors wouldn't release me to go back to work, and the hand surgeon had said I wouldn't be able to work because of my hands. I talked to my family, and they said I needed to talk to the social worker that had come to the house. She hadn't been able to help before because I couldn't remember anything and neither my family nor I could find any of my records so that I could have information to give her.

I searched and searched, and I couldn't find any records. I decided to stop for a few days and start looking again. I finally found them in the back of my car. No one had even thought to look there. Why they were in the back of my car, I still do not know. I realized then there was not any money anywhere to draw from. I started panicking, not knowing what to do. I called the social worker. She told me that I needed to go to social services and to ask them for food stamps and a Medicare card, in case I couldn't pay for my Blue Cross policy. My employer might not carry me very long on Blue Cross, or they might let me go, and I definitely needed insurance. She also told me I needed to go right away to social security and apply for disability, because you had to wait six months for that, and they did not give you the money for the first six months.

The first place that I went to was Social Services, and even though people were very nice there, I still felt very humiliated about accepting aid. I had been working since I was fourteen and couldn't fathom that I would ever have to go there and ask for help. Although I had no money in savings and no money in checking, I still had a life insurance policy that was worth $2,100.00, and if you had anything worth $2,000.00, you had to cash it in, in order to be eligible. I did not want to do that because I wasn't sure I was going to survive. I could not get another life insurance policy, because of the transplant, and I wanted to be sure that Shawn would have money to go to college, if I did not survive. The policy would pay $50,000.00. I was worried about having another rejection, and the hospital not being able to stop it, and another organ not being available. There was a high percent chance that there would not be another organ available should I need it.

I couldn't figure out what I was going to do and how I was going to make it, but I explained to the social worker that I couldn't cash in the policy because I might not survive and my son needed to go to college. I explained that I knew his father would not pay for his college so I needed to be sure that he would have money to at least go two years. The social worker said she would talk to her supervisor and see if there's anything that they could do, but unless I gave that up, she did not think I would be eligible for either a medical card or for food stamps or for any other financial help. She told me that I would be receiving a letter in the mail telling me what they had decided to do. I understood that there were rules and laws to abide, but I couldn't understand why I had worked all those years and had nothing now, yet they couldn't see why I needed to keep the life insurance policy.

Next I went to Social Security and had to wait a couple of hours in order to get in to see someone. By the time I got in, I was very tired and not feeling well. I just hoped that I could remember everything they needed to know. But, when I did get in to see someone and explained the situation, they were very, very helpful. They helped me fill out the forms, because I couldn't figure it out myself. I didn't have all the information with me that they needed, but they said they could get all the information from my employer and from the hospital.

As I walked out of that office, I didn't know what I was going to do. I didn't want to ask anybody for help, but I did not want to lose everything either. How was I going to make my house payment and my car payment? How was I going to feed my son? How was I going to give him lunch money? I truly had no idea at that point what I was going to do. Bill had contacted my employer, who had contacted worker's comp, but they were fighting against giving me money, even though they had sent me to the doctor who had given me the medication that had started this whole spiral of events.

A few of my friends came to visit me and asked me how it was going. Even though it hurt my pride and ego to tell them, I explained the financial situation and that I didn't know what I was going to do. One of them happened to work at a bank and told me that I could ask the bank to let me make interest-only payments for my house and car while I was recuperating. I should explain the situation to them, and let them know that within six months I would probably have money coming from social security. I could also ask them for a home equity loan, because I had been paying for my house for thirteen years and should have a lot of equity in it. I was so grateful that even though I did not have the ability to come up with solutions at that time, I was lucky to have friends who could help me figure something out. The next day I did go to the bank, and I was able to get a home equity loan, and I did not have to start paying it back for a few months after that. So, I was able to look ahead and be able to see that I was not going to lose my home or my car, and I was going to be able to take care of my son. Eventually I should be able to get money from Social Security, Social Services or Worker's Compensation.

I was pleasantly surprised a few weeks later to get food stamps and a Medicare card from Social Services. I didn't get a letter stating anything about my case, but I did get the benefits. I was really surprised because they had thought that I wouldn't be eligible, and I thought to myself, "They must have found a way. My guardian angel is looking after me again." I had always thought that I had a great guardian angel. Ever since I had managed to get away from my father and be on my own, my life had been pretty good. I figured there always had been a guardian angel there to help me out. Any time I needed to make decisions in my life, they came pretty easy and most of them were right. So I thought, *Great, my guardian angel is back. That's what I need. I need somebody else on my side.*

I was still seeing my therapist every week, and he was always coming up with ways to help me try to cope with the situation. He wanted me to write in a journal every day, which I did. He encouraged me to write down all my thoughts, whether they were good or bad. And in one particular session, he said to me, "Have you seen your family, since they've gone back to West Virginia and Virginia?" and I told him, "No." He said, "Well, why don't you go see them? Since your neurologist has been able to control the seizures with medication, you know you can drive now, right?" And I told him, "Yes, of course I can drive. I drive here all the time." He said, "Well, maybe you could make the trip." I explained to him that it was eight hours to get there. He suggested that maybe I try driving two hours and stopping, driving another two hours and stopping at a hotel for the night, and then driving the other four hours the next day, stopping again after two hours. I couldn't imagine this, because I still felt like such an invalid, but he was so encouraging. He said, "Look if you can't do it, turn around and come back." That's the way he always was. He was always coming up with things that I would never have thought of doing yet.

I decided since Thanksgiving was in a week, maybe I would try it then. I talked to Bill and asked him if he wanted to go with me, but he couldn't since he had been off work so long caring for me. Since he'd gone back to his job, he was really trying to make up for all the money that he had lost while taking care of me. He thought maybe it would be better if I didn't go. I told him that I really wanted to try and he finally agreed with me, but he warned me to not overdo it and if I became too tired, that I promise him that I would turn around and come back.

My family were so surprised when I called and told them that I was actually going to try to drive down there for Thanksgiving. They were the most critical of all. They asked me if I was sure that I even wanted to try it and they asked why Bill wasn't coming. They thought that I should wait until he could bring me. They were just amazed that I was even going to try it. I explained to them that I was getting better and that they would know that when they saw me. I told them that the hospital had lowered my medication dosage and changed the ones that gave me the worst side effects so I could function better. I told them that I did not look as bad, and that I was trying to get healthier and that I was eating exactly what I should. They finally agreed that I should try and they were thrilled that I was actually going to come to see them.

A few days after I decided to go to West Virginia to see my family, Bill encouraged me to get a dog to take with me. He told me that I should not be traveling alone. A dog could keep me company, because he was working so many hours and Shawn was involved in a lot of activities. I told him that I did not want the responsibility of taking care of a dog, but then he told me that, in Michigan they only keep animals in the Humane Society for a couple of weeks and then they put them to sleep because they can't afford to keep them. That encouraged me to get one, and I did adopt a dog that had been very, very abused. He hadn't been adoptable because many people felt that he would have a lot of problems. He seemed so sad and he seemed like physically he didn't feel well either. I thought, "Wow, what a good match we will be."

Adopting Brutus was one of the best things I did during my period of recovery although I felt sorry for that dog because I smothered him so much. I had such a fear of negative things around me, that I was afraid that the dog might die, and I didn't think I could handle that. So I kept that dog with me everywhere I went. The poor dog, I thought that sometimes he just wanted to be left alone but he went along with whatever I wanted to do and wherever I wanted to go. He seemed to want to be around me most of the time. I really think that he and I actually helped each other get better.

I did go to West Virginia for Thanksgiving. It took me two days to get there, and two days to get back, but I was able to spend three or four days there. However, I had a big fear of being away from the hospital too long and had to go back. My family would have loved it had I stayed longer, but I just couldn't. I felt unsafe away from the hospital. I felt like I had to be there just in case my blood work was bad and they needed me to come in immediately. I was still battling with that big fear of having rejections.

Christmas that year was a lot different than it had been in the past. I did not have a lot of money, like I used to have, so I couldn't get Shawn all the different presents that I wanted to. But, he seemed okay with that. He was just glad that we were back at home together, that he was around his friends and at the school where all his friends were going.

Chapter 23

ABOUT SIX MONTHS AFTER MY TRANSPLANT, MY SON SEEMED TO be acting differently. I couldn't figure out what it was that was different about him. His behavior seemed to be changing. He wasn't the happy-go-lucky kid that he had always been. He always looked so serious, and his grades were dropping. Sometimes I would say something to him, and he would answer me back in a tone that I had never heard before. It was like he was angry with me, and I couldn't figure out why. He knew that it wasn't my fault that I had been ill. I don't know whether he still was having the big fear that I was going to die, or if he just wanted the mother that he had always had.

Maybe it was because I looked so different. Even though I was feeling better, I didn't look well. Maybe it was because we had had such a drastic change in our lives. In looking at it from his point of view, he used to have a mother who would get up every morning, get dressed, grab her briefcase and her laptop, and out the door she'd go. She would go to work, pick him up after work, have dinner with him, they would go to the business that she owned, and then they would come home. Now he had a mother that was still in bed in the morning when he went to school. When he got home from school, she didn't look anything like she used to look, and she was always tired. He knew that financially we had a lot less money than we used to.

I don't think it was the financial situation. I think Shawn had adapted to that problem. But I really think he was having problems because his whole life had turned upside down. His father and I had divorced when he was two years old, so I had been the parent that he had been with most of the time. I felt that must be why he was changing so drastically, because his security in life was so shaken.

Next, the school counselor called me and asked me to come in, and she said that my son's grades were falling even more, and that he was fighting with other students, and that he didn't seem very happy, and that she was very concerned about him. I explained the situation to her, what had happened to us, and how our life had so traumatically changed. She suggested that perhaps Shawn should live with his father for a while. I explained to her that his father had not spent a lot of time with him during his childhood. And she said, "Well maybe it is about time he and his father got to know each other better, and maybe they can help each other. Maybe they can get closer as a father and a son, and also maybe his father can help him accept what has happened to you."

Shawn was very unhappy with my decision, but his father agreed to it, and so he did go live with his father. He did not talk to me for a long time after that, but I did feel it was better for him, because I felt like his father could take better care of him during that time than I could. I also thought that I could get better a lot faster if I didn't always have to pretend I was okay when I wasn't. If I could rest when I needed to rest, instead of just resting during the day, and pretending to be okay in the evenings when my son was at home, I could get better faster.

Shawn was so upset with me, but I did eventually talk him into talking to a counselor who worked exclusively with teenagers. I explained to him that never in my life had I thought that I would have to talk to a therapist, and that probably he didn't feel that way either. I told him that I would really like him to go see this person, because he could talk to him and he could say anything to him that he wanted, just like I had, and that it would all be confidential.

I told Shawn I really wanted him to do that before he came home, so maybe he'd have a better understanding of how to cope with what had happened to us. He didn't agree at first, but finally he did and he went to see the therapist for about a month. After that the therapist told me that he thought my son was ready to come home again and that had gained a better understanding of what had happened. The therapist said that he thought he had been able to help him, giving him different ideas about how to cope with the fact that our life had changed and how to cope with other things that might happen in the future. He said if Shawn needed to talk to him again, he could come in and see him, just to give him a call.

Chapter 24

I HAD GOTTEN MYSELF INTO A ROUTINE AT HOME. I WAS FORCING myself to get out of the house. I was using the same routine that my family had used when they were trying to get me better. I was doing all the things that they did for me and I was doing them by myself. For exercise I was going to a park and walking as much as I could each day to try to get healthier and lose weight. My hair was growing back, so it didn't look so bad. My face wasn't quite as big, because they had lowered the dosage a little more on the steroid that they were giving me and my face wasn't as swollen all the time.

Sometimes things would seem to be progressing well and then something would happen that would put me back again. The hospital had kept reiterating that transplant patients at first take one step forward and three back, then two steps forward and two back and so on until eventually you will be going forward and very seldom going backward. After one of those occasions, when I was feeling that I was going backward too many steps, I started to believe that something bad or evil was causing these things to happen to me. I was in my back yard and I actually looked toward the sky and said, "Just bring it on, because after all that I have had to handle in the last few months, I can handle anything that you can throw at me." As crazy as it sounds, I still wish that I had not said that because of what happened next.

One of my friends encouraged me to go back and start having my hair done and maybe that would make me feel better. I made an appointment with the lady who had been doing my hair for years. "How ironic." I thought to myself, because her little boy had received the first living donor adult to child liver transplant in Michigan. The little boy's father had given him part of his liver, because the little boy had been born with a liver that wasn't functioning.

She already knew what had happened to me because her aunt was my friend who had come to Bill's house and taken me out to the store to buy thank you cards for all the people who had sent me cards, called me, or come to see me. She thought I looked pretty good, considering that I was still on the steroid, because her little boy had been on it for many, many years, and his face had stayed big all that time. Halfway through cutting my hair, she stopped, and she was holding the back of my hair up in her hand. I looked in the mirror and I could see by the look on her face that something was terribly wrong, so I asked her what it was.

She looked at me strangely and in a voice with a hint of sadness in it, told me that she needed to talk to me alone in another part of the salon. I went back there with dread in my heart, because I could feel that this was not going to be something that I wanted to hear or to cope with. She told me that I was losing my hair that I might lose part of it or I might lose all of it. There was no way for her to know. She told me that I had a disease called alopecia. She said that her little boy had had it right after he'd had his transplant, but that his hair had grown back within six months. She said it wasn't something that transplant patients usually had, but that two million people in the world currently had it. There was no known reason for it, except that they knew everyone who had it had gone through either a major trauma, a major surgery, or had had on-going stress. "Great." I said to her, "I have all of those things happening. How can it be cured?" And she said to me what was one of the worst sentences I have ever heard in my life, "There is no cure, because they are not sure what happened to cause it in the first place." She said, "You will just have to wait and see what happens." She said, "I must warn you, though, it might take a long, long time for it to come out. For my little boy it was nothing, because he didn't know it was happening."

She said, "I have had many clients who have come in and I've had to tell them, because I'm the first one to see what's happening; at first the hair comes out in small circles so they cannot see it themselves." It comes out little by little and they may lose it just on the top of their head or they may lose it all. It could take six months before it stopped coming out or it was all gone. She said that some people had gotten it back and some others never got it back. People who lose their hair from cancer treatments such as chemo or radiation almost always get it back, but it was not the same with ones who lost it for other reasons, although it was not impossible for it to come back. She said there were many types of alopecia and there was no way of knowing which type I had. She suggested I go to the dermatologist at the hospital right away and show him what she had found. They could start some different treatments that might help me. She said although there was no known cure, there were some treatments that could keep it from getting worse.

I was surprised that I did not cry at that time. I went into a state of shock and I didn't talk to anyone for two days. When I washed my hair I realized, looking down in the shower, how much of it was coming out. I tried not to wash my hair too often, because every time I would wash it and see how much was gone I would not talk to anyone or go out of my house for days. It was coming out in clumps. Even when I just got my head wet, the hair would fall out.

I did make an appointment with the dermatologist. He was very familiar with it, but he also said the same thing my hair stylist had told me, that there really was no cure. There were some different treatments that he could try to stop it, and if I were willing to go through them, he would try. I decided that I would do just about anything to stop all my hair from falling out.

I then started having the same recurring nightmare concerning my hair. Ever since my transplant, I had only had a few nightmares, but had a lot of flashbacks. I have talked to a lot of Vietnam veterans in my life who told me that they had flashbacks and would describe them to me, but no matter how hard I tried to understand what they meant when they were telling me, I really had no idea until I was having them myself. I would be sitting somewhere and I would flash back to when I was in the coma and could not come out of it. It was just as real as when it had actually happened.

At other times, I would flash back to the second in the coma that I believed was when I had the stroke. That was when I felt such intense heat sweep completely up and down my body. I would be doing something and I would suddenly feel the exact same feeling of heat. I mostly went back to the time in the coma when I saw myself from above, of looking down at myself, and saw myself lying on a bed with absolutely no hair. And I thought to myself, "Was that a premonition? Was that something you were supposed to remember, so that you could deal with it now when your hair is actually falling out?" Or, was it that something dark and evil had shown me what was going to happen to me when I was in the coma and now it was coming true. I had totally forgotten about it until now. Then I remembered, so clearly, that I had absolutely no hair at all, anywhere on my body. But I said to myself, "Wait, I'm just losing my hair on my head. I still have hair on my legs, under my arms and everywhere else. So maybe, I won't lose all my hair." But I still had that fear, and I kept having the flashback about it. That is when the recurring nightmares started. I would go to sleep at night and wake up in a cold sweat because I kept seeing myself in the dream lying there with no hair anywhere.

It took five slow agonizing months for the nightmare to become true and a reality, but all of my hair did fall out. It not only fell out on my head, but it fell off all over my entire body. The dermatologist tried everything. He tried shots in my scalp. He tried different salves to put on my head. He actually gave me a prescription one time for something new, but when I went to the pharmacist they gave me the wrong strength of the prescription, and it burnt the skin off of the top of my head. Instead of giving me .01 amount of the medication, they gave me the one that was .10, so it was ten times stronger than what the dermatologist had intended and it burned me.

When I was at home being depressed about my hair, I went through many, many days and nights of crying. I kept telling myself to quit feeling sorry for myself and just be grateful to be alive. I would be okay until I woke up in the morning and clumps of hair would be on my pillow, or I would take a shower and see the hair all around me. It was so devastating. I was still thankful about everything else, but I had always tried to look the best that I could, so this was hard for me. I did research it on the Internet concerning alopecia and indeed there were two million people in the world that had it, and many people who did not ever get their hair back.

I actually joined a support group on line, to support each other, and to talk to and encourage each other. It didn't seem to help me very much, except that one of the people on line suggested that I take some of the hair from my hairbrush, before it fell out completely so that I could have wigs made that would match my hair exactly. I was so defeated by this. I was back to wearing a scarf on my head, but I realized I couldn't wear a scarf forever, that I needed to suck it up and go to a wig shop and buy a wig.

The first wig place that I went to, I explained to them what had happened about my hair. They were very nice to me, and they wanted to see a picture of me before. So I made another appointment, and I came back and showed them a picture and showed them the sample of my hair and they were able to make a wig up that looked very close to my hair. The problem was that you could tell it was a wig. Or at least I could tell it was a wig, and it was heavy and it was hot and it was uncomfortable. But I did wear it, because it was better than walking around with no hair or wearing scarves all the time.

Shawn never commented about all this, as if he wanted to pretend like it was never happening. However, Bill was very funny about it. He actually said to me, "Hey, get a bunch of different wigs. It'd be like being with a different person every day." He tried to find humor in it. I was so glad that he loved me so much that it didn't matter. I think it mattered most because of vanity. I was having such a hard time coping with it.

But something kept lingering in my mind; something that I thought might help me. Then I realized what it was. By that time it was a year after my transplant and the hospital had taken me off of the steroid drug, because I'd had so many side effects from it. One of the side effects was that I had a lot of facial hair and I had really thick hair on my arms and on my legs. So I called the dermatologist immediately and suggested that maybe I could try taking the steroid again. But he said, "You know, they took you off of it because you had all these side effects." And I said, "I'm willing to live with the side effects, if I can have my hair back." So he told me he would talk to my transplant team, and see if they could put me on a low dose of the drug.

The transplant team agreed to after I went to talk to them and explained to them, for my own mental health, to please let me try. So they had agreed to it. It was amazing. Within a month my hair started growing back. But the strange thing about it was, whereas my hair was light brown and straight previously, it was now black and very, very curly. When I asked the dermatologist about this, he explained to me that if you lose your hair and you somehow get it to come back that you pick up a different hair gene. Whereas before I probably had my mother's hair gene, I now had my father's hair gene. But it didn't matter to me, as long as I had hair back. I was thrilled to have hair back. Not only just for the looks, but because I was so much more comfortable.

However, I was not meant to have it, because within five or six months of having my hair back, the drug started giving me even more side effects than when I was on it before. I became diabetic again. I was having vision problems. I had acne again on my face and my chest and my back. I was unable to sleep at night. Even though I was on a smaller dose, it didn't matter. The dermatologist had to break the news to me that he was so sorry, but he had to take me off of it again. He said that it wasn't in my best interest health-wise to stay on it. They knew I wanted to have my hair, but that my health was more important at that point than my hair.

Just a few weeks after going off the steroid, all my hair fell out again. About the time, the support group on the Internet had started talking about the fact that there were companies that were making a hair replacement that was not just a wig, but a prosthetic. They would actually mold your head and make a cap out of soft synthetic breathable material, and then they would integrate hair into it and make it into a different kind of wig. When you put it on your head and pushed it down, it would actually vacuum to your head. That way when you were out in the wind or something, the prosthetic would stay in place and no one would ever know that it was a wig. It was so much more comfortable without having the elastic band that went around your head on a wig.

I contacted my health insurance company, who were covering my medical care until worker's comp would start covering it, but they told me that they did not cover those. They said they had never heard of them and not only that, they did not cover wigs either. Previously I had paid for the wigs myself, because I didn't even think about using my medical insurance, but the support group on line were talking about the fact that some of their insurances would pay for the prosthetic, because it was a prosthetic, just like an artificial arm or leg. We would just be getting a hair prosthetic.

A few months later an attorney's office called me and told me that pretty soon it was time for my trial. I vaguely remembered talking to an attorney when I was very, very ill. They told me that my family had signed papers for me, because the worker's compensation company was fighting me as far as giving me income and covering my medical expenses. So after going through depositions and talking to my attorneys and actually going through a trial, I was able to get worker's compensation. In addition, the judge had said that they had to pay for anything that was pertaining to my transplant. I then submitted to them that I wanted to get a prosthetic, and was very happy when they agreed to pay for it.

The only company that anyone knew about was in California. When I contacted the company in California, they told me within a month they would be in the area where I lived, and that they could see me and do a mold of my head and get one started for me. I was thrilled. It seemed like such a good answer to the problem. It took months to get the prosthetic, but I was okay waiting, because I knew eventually that it would come. The lady who had molded my head was the owner of the company, and she had had alopecia and no hair since she was a teenager. She knew exactly how I felt, and that's why she made such good products, because she wore her own product herself and had been since she first designed it in her early twenties. She used real hair and only used the most beautiful hair, so that the hair that she had put in my prosthetic was more beautiful than my own had been.

Chapter 25

THIS WHOLE EPISODE ABOUT THE PROSTHETIC WAS encouraging because it made me realize that if I tried hard enough I could come up with a solution for almost anything. If I just kept at it and made it a goal to come up with solutions, then I would find them. The hair loss problem was one problem that I had not asked God to help me with because he had already done so much for me that I didn't want to ask for anything else. I knew there were people in the world that had cancer and other terminal illnesses and figured he would want to help them before helping me concerning my hair growing back. I think he was looking out for me though because I was starting to accept what had happened to me quicker than I thought I would. I knew I would go through bouts of depression from time to time, but it was great just spending more time with Shawn.

Currently I was okay financially. I was making my bills, and that's all I wanted to do. I was just happy doing that. A year later a malpractice lawsuit went through the courts that my family had also filed. And even though there was a ceiling on how much money I could get, I was very lucky to get enough money to have a second transplant. As long as I knew that I had the money for a second transplant, then I felt secure. I had been worrying so much that I wouldn't have the money to have a second one. Now I could see farther ahead in my life, and see perhaps that if I had two transplants, I would be able to live at least twenty more years.

I was not able to return to my job. My employer eventually did let me go. They said that they didn't have any jobs that I could do because of the memory loss and also not being able to use my hands. Because the anti-rejection medications that I had to take for life wiped out my immune system, I was always getting every cold, virus, flu, that came along, so I was sick most of the winters in Michigan. Two of my friends suggested that I go to Florida with them to visit their parents who lived in the Florida Keys. They wanted me to see how warm it was there all year round and that their parents were rarely ill because of living there. Eventually I was able to live in Florida most of the winters, and it did cut down on the times that I became very ill.

Although the medication that I'm on, and will be on forever, still makes me extremely tired at times, and unable to have a regular job, I still am happy with my life. I have found things to do in my life that are rewarding. Raising my son was one of the most rewarding things that I have ever done. And even though I was ill a lot, I still had more time for him. He went to college four years for computers, has a good job, recently bought his own home and is planning to get married. Because of seeing the example of my faith in God, he now relies on God to help him with his life too.

One of the most memorable moments in my life that I cannot think about without crying is the day that Shawn came to me and told me that he had decided to give me part of his liver when I needed a second transplant. He said that Karen had told him about living donor adult liver transplants and he had researched it extensively on the Internet. He said if we were the same blood type and we were both pretty healthy at the time, they would take the left side of his liver out and put it in me. Within a few weeks, the part that had been cut out of him would grow back and I would be able to function with the half they had put in me. I let him explain it to me in detail because he was so excited about it and I was so touched. I already knew everything he was saying and I talked about it when I did public speaking about transplants. He was so happy that this was a possibility.

I currently work with people the hospital at the top of a transplant list who are waiting, and I try to encourage them to hold on. I tell them I had only two hours to live when I had my transplant. Everyone had given up hope, even the doctors had told my family they should probably tell me goodbye, that I was not going to make it, but I did get a transplant. I tell these people to hang in there, because every day medical research is learning more. I also tell them that every day more and more people are becoming organ donors. Almost every person I have talked to and explained that they can save a life, or in some manner make life better for fifty-two people has decided to become an organ donor. Every day the anti-rejection drugs are getting better. I tell them to hang in there, to keep having faith in God or a higher being, that they will make it.

I am currently part of a support group that is for both people who are waiting for transplants, and people who have already had transplants. They can bring their family members. This seems to be a very good thing, because everyone can talk about everything that's on his or her mind and there is someone there who understands what he or she is saying. Some family members cannot understand what their loved one is going through because they have not experienced it themselves, so it is good to have another transplant recipient who totally understands.

We can be angry, especially those of us who did not cause our organs to fail due to alcohol or drugs, or those of us who were born with an organ problem or those of us who had a blood transfusion before the time that blood was checked for hepatitis. Nobody judges us there because they know we will only be angry for a short time and then we will feel grateful again. I have worked with many family members who are just as angry as the organ transplant recipients because their loved one has to go through so much. I have found if the person has caused this to happen to them and are lucky enough to get a transplant, they are not as angry as the rest of us.

The very most important thing I do is to be a volunteer public speaker for an organization called Gift of Life. When I first started doing public speaking for this organization, half as many people died waiting for transplants as actually received them every year. So if 10,000 people that year received transplants, there were 5,000 other people who died waiting. Fortunately these numbers have changed. They have gotten somewhat better, but still it's tragic to think about how many people die each year.

In the United States currently, there are 99,000 people waiting for transplants. There are millions of people who die each year in the United States. If just 100,000 of those people per year were organ donors, then no one would have to die waiting. That is why it has become my goal in life to make others aware of the vital importance of being an organ donor. Even though I don't have a job like everyone else, and even though I don't have a great deal of money, I know that this is my purpose in life. My purpose is to explain how I would never have survived and never have been able to raise my son and never have been able to have such a good life had it not been for organ donation.

Chapter 26

I WOULD LIKE TO END THIS BOOK WITH A TRIBUTE TO MY ORGAN donor and his family. My transplant would not have happened if it were not for a 17-year old boy in Indiana who was always doing something to help others during all his short life. His name was Justin Scott. When his parents were asked if they would donate his organs, they did not hesitate because they knew that was what Justin would have wanted. I thank God for these parents who honored what they knew their son's wishes would be.

Even though the parents thought the decision to donate was the right one, it was an especially hard one for the mother, Debbie Scott. Nine years after the transplant, she was finally able to contact me. I had sent a few thank you notes during the first two years after my transplant and when there was no response, I stopped because I somehow knew in my heart that I was just reminding the family and probably causing them more pain each time I sent a note.

When correspondence first starts between a recipient and the donor family, it has to be done by letters sent to The Gift of Life Agency. The Gift of Life reads them to be sure that they are okay and then forwards them to the other party. When The Gift of Life determines that it is okay for the two parties to communicate with each other directly, they release the address, phone number, etc. that one party wants the other to have.

Debbie told me that she wrote me a note each year, but just could not send them. I totally understand that because if it had been my son who had died, I don't know if I could ever contact the recipient because it would be a reminder too painful to deal with. From talking to other donor families, each family is different in the way they handle being able to or not being able to have a relationship with the recipient.

My first conversation with Debbie was by phone and lasted for three hours. I was so afraid that I would say something to her to make her wish that she had not donated her son's organs. I decided to just be myself and hope for the best. She said that it was wonderful to talk to me and that she was happy to know how grateful I was to have gotten her son's liver. When I explained to her that if it were not for the donation that I would not be alive, I think she realized just how grateful I was for my life.

She asked for a photo of me and I requested a photo from her of Justin. I wanted a photo to use in my talks about organ donation. I wanted to honor Justin by showing his picture to everyone that I talked to. Justin and his mother spent a lot of time together outdoors hiking and camping. She said that Justin loved any kind of sport and especially fishing. She said that when he and his friends were bored, Justin would always come up with an idea of something to do. One of the things I learned about Justin that was so heartwarming was his decision to shave his head if necessary in order to raise money for another boy who needed cancer treatment. It means so much to me to know these things about Justin because I could always sense the kind of person he was even before I talked to his mother.

My donor, Justin Scott, had a sister named Lacey who was sixteen when he died and now, nine years later, she has two beautiful children, Alivia and Ruston. I am in the process of making plans to go to Indiana and meet the family and friends of my donor. It will be very hard at first because all I will want to do is cry for the loss they have endured. The one thing that I cling to is something that Debbie wrote to me in a letter. She said that I have become everything she never knew she wanted a recipient to be.

This means a lot to me and makes me more determined to do everything in my power to make this liver last as long as I can before needing another transplant. It will be eleven years in just a few months since my transplant and my monthly blood work shows my liver functions are perfect. Other tests that are run on my blood are perfect as well.

I also want to thank my therapist, Michael Rozich and my psychologist, Dr. Debra Nagy, who so encouraged me to write this book. They knew that it would help me move forward in a positive way. Most importantly, I want to thank God for always being there for me.

Resources About Transplants and Organ Donation

website	organization	description
www.unos.org	United Network for Organ Sharing	network of doctors, patients, researchers and general public
www.organdonor.gov	OrganDonor.gov	US Government information about organ donation
www.livingdonorsonline.org	International Association of Living Organ Donors, Inc.	information about forms of living donation
www.ustransplant.org	The Scientific Registry of Transplant Recipients	national database of statistics related to solid organ transplantation
www.uktransplant.org	UK Transplant	United Kingdom National Health Service donor registry
www.transplants.org	National Foundation for Transplants (NFT)	Financial Aid for transplants
www.transplantliving.org	Transplant Living	information for patients, including financing information
www.livingdonors.org	National Kidney Foundation	NKF concerning living donors
www.transplantspeakers.org	Transplant Speakers International	speakers about transplants and organ donation
www.transweb.org/comet	National Council On Minority Education in Transplantation	raising awareness of the minority community to organ and tissue donation
www.cota.org	Children's Organ Transplant Association	funding assistance and family support for children and young adults needing transplant
www.cherubs.org	Children's Helpers Educating, Reassuring and Uniting By Sharing	Raising awareness about child organ donation
www.transplantexperience.com	Transplant Experience	Information and support for patients
www.giftoflifemichigan.org	Gift of Life, Michigan	Michigan donor registry
www.trioweb.org	Transplant Recipients International Organization (TRIO)	for transplant candidates, recipients, their families and the families of donors
www.americanheart.org	American Heart Association	Information about heart health
www.lungusa.org	American Lung Association	Informaiton about lung health
www.liverfoundation.org	American Liver Foundation	Information about liver health
www.kidney.org	National Kidney Foundation	Information about kidney disease and treatment, including transplant
www.intestinaltransplant.org	Intestinal Transplant Registry	concerning bowel transplantation
www.marrow.org	National Marrow Donor Program	supporting bone marrow transplant